Triple Goddess Bulb Pl[...]
for Flowers that are E[...]
and Magical as [...]

D0118413

Take the bulbs that you want to plant and the bulb planting tool to the garden.
Dig the holes, then place the bulbs in the earth, while chanting:

Seasons change—the Wheel turns 'round—
Bulbs, I plant you in the ground.
Dormant bulbs, you'll come alive,
And when the Spring comes, sprout and thrive.

As you cover the bulbs with soil, chant:

Goddess Maiden, dance and play
Upon this soil throughout the day.
Crone so wise, so gnarled and old
Work magical mysteries in darkest cold.
Goddess Mother, give them birth
So they sprout and thrive upon the Earth—
And let them blossom wild and free
The Wheel turns 'round! So mote it be!

Water the bulbs well. Repeat the last chant once a day until the first bulb
sprouts.

About the Author

Dorothy Morrison is a Wiccan High Priestess of the Georgian Tradition. She founded the Coven of the Crystal Garden in 1986. An avid practitioner of the Ancient Arts for more than twenty years, she teaches the Craft to students throughout the United States and Australia and is a member of the Pagan Poet's Society.

An archer and bow hunter, Dorothy regularly competes in outdoor tournaments and holds titles in several states. Her other interests include Tarot work, magical herbalism, stonework, and computer networking.

To Write to the Author

If you wish to contact the author or would like more information about this book, please write to the author in care of Llewellyn Worldwide and we will forward your request. Both the author and publisher appreciate hearing from you and learning of your enjoyment of this book and how it has helped you. Llewellyn Worldwide cannot guarantee that every letter written to the author can be answered, but all will be forwarded. Please write to:

Dorothy Morrison
℅ Llewellyn Worldwide
P.O. Box 64383, Dept. 1-56718-443-X
St. Paul, MN 55164-0383, U.S.A.

Please enclose a self-addressed stamped envelope for reply, or $1.00 to cover costs. If outside U.S.A., enclose international postal reply coupon.

Many of Llewellyn's authors have websites with additional information and resources. For more information, please visit our website at
http://www.llewellyn.com

Bud, Blossom, & Leaf

The Magical Herb Gardener's Handbook

Dorothy Morrison

2004

Llewellyn Publications

St. Paul, Minnesota 55164-0383, U.S.A.

Bud, Blossom, & Leaf: The Magical Herb Gardener's Handbook © 2001 by Dorothy Morrison. All rights reserved. No part of this book may be used or reproduced in any manner whatsoever, including Internet usage, without written permission from Llewellyn Publications except in the case of brief quotations embodied in critical articles and reviews.

FIRST EDITION
Third Printing, 2004

Cover design by Lisa Novak
Cover photograph by Doug Deutscher
Herbal consultant: Elizabeth Ann Johnson
Interior illustrations by Nyease Somersett

Library of Congress Cataloging-in-Publication Data
Morrison, Dorothy, 1955–
Bud, blossom & leaf: the magical herb gardener's handbook / Dorothy Morrison.
p. cm.
Includes bibliographical references (p.).
ISBN 1-56718-443-X
1. Herb gardening. 2. Herbs. 3. Herbs—Utilization.
I. Title: Bud, blossom, and leaf. II. Title.

SB351.H5 M667 2001
635'.7—dc21   00-048144

Llewellyn Worldwide does not participate in, endorse, or have any authority or responsibility concerning private business transactions between our authors and the public.
All mail addressed to the author is forwarded but the publisher cannot, unless specifically instructed by the author, give out an address or phone number.

Llewellyn Publications
A Division of Llewellyn Worldwide, Ltd.
P.O. Box 64383, Dept. 1-56718-443-X
St. Paul, MN 55164-0383, U.S.A.
www.llewellyn.com

Portions of this book contain herbal remedies, recipes, and suggestions for magical use. The purpose of this book is to provide educational, cultural, and historical information for the general public concerning herbal remedies that have been used for many centuries. In offering information, the author and publisher assume no responsibility for self-diagnosis based on these studies or traditional uses of herbs in the past. Some herbs and remedies discussed in this book involve toxic or potentially dangerous materials, and the publisher takes no position on the beliefs or effectiveness of methods or treatments discussed in *Bud, Blossom, & Leaf.*

♻ Printed on recycled paper in the United States of America

To Sue Crossen, who, like the Maiden in Her twirling Spring Dance,
nurtured, fertilized, nudged, and willed the seeds of this project
to grow until they sprouted and blossomed into reality;
and to her family, Jim, Cody, and Tim,
for sharing this remarkable woman with me.

Other Books by Dorothy Morrison

Magical Needlework
Llewellyn Publications, 1998

Everyday Magic
Llewellyn Publications, 1998

In Praise of the Crone: A Celebration of Feminine Maturity
Llewellyn Publications, 1999

The Whimsical Tarot
Deck and book; U.S. Games Systems Inc., 2000

Yule: A Celebration of Light & Warmth
Llewellyn Publications, 2000

The Craft: A Witch's Book of Shadows
Llewellyn Publications, 2001

The Craft Companion: A Witch's Journal
Llewellyn Publications, 2001

Everyday Tarot Magic: Meditation & Spells
Llewellyn Publications, 2003

Everyday Moon Magic: Spells & Rituals for Abundant Living
Llewellyn Publications, 2004

Contents

Preface   xi
Acknowledgments   xiii

Part One: Mother Nature's Playground

Planning, Locating, and Preparing   3

Initializing the Magic; Magical Garden Themes; Shapes, Symbolism, and Magical Portents; Harmonizing with Your Climate; Herbs Need Friends, Too; Sizing the Magic; Choosing an Outdoor Gardening Spot; Gardening Permission Ritual; Compost Recipe; Choosing an Indoor Gardening Location; Home Spirit Help Ritual; Starting Seedlings Indoors; Blessing the Seeds; Sterilizing the Soil; Cleansing Pots and Containers; More Seed Planting Preparations; Protection for Sprouts and Seedlings

Learning, Turning, and Discerning   29

Tools of the Trade; Tool Consecration; Marking the Outdoor Garden Area; Turning, Tilling, and Playing in the Dirt; The Thanksgiving Ritual; Invoke the Spring Ritual; Mother Nature's Weather Predictions; Windsock Workings; The Winds; Thinning and Strengthening; The Cold Frame; Getting Started Indoors: Working with Moon Phases and Moon Signs; The Strawberry Pot; Gardening with Hydroponics; The Hydroponic System; Conventional Potting; Compost Tea; Magical Help for Indoor Plants; The Balancing Act; Dealing

with Pesky Critters; Mole, Gopher, and Field Mouse Begone
Ritual; Rabbit and Deer Away Ritual; Bird Flyaway Ritual;
Purchased Plants: How to Find Healthy Ones; Transplanting
Seedlings Outdoors; Garden Blessing Ritual; Alternative Gar-
den Blessing Ritual

Growing, Hoeing, & Keeping Things Going   61

Give the Garden a Drink; Giving Herbs Some Breathing Room;
To Mulch or Not to Mulch; Herbs Need Snacks and TLC; The
Gardeners' Rede: Pull That Weed; Waging the War on Flying,
Crawling, and Creeping Critters; Heavy Artillery; Fighting Flea-
bane Formula; Wormwood Warlord Formula; Screaming Ban-
shee Formula; Basil Bomber Formula; Garlic Guerrilla For-
mula; Waging the War on Slime; Beer Trap; Tube Trap; The
Horticultural Medic; Fungus Among Us; Chamomile Fungal
Remedy; Horsetail Fungal Remedy; Old-Fashioned Fungal
Remedy; Garden Meditation; Harvesting the Bounty; Harvest
Thanksgiving Ritual; Preparing the Harvest; Herb Drying Tech-
niques; Storing Fresh Herbs; Plant Propagation Methods; Start-
ing Cuttings; Living Herb Wreath; Starting Plants by Layering;
Procreation by Division; Planting Fall Bulbs; Bulb Planting
Spell; Putting the Garden to Bed; Giving the Garden a Blanket

Part Two: Mother Nature's Household

After the Harvest   95

General Enchantment Notes; About the House

Herbal Pest Control   99

Ants; Flies; Mice and Rats; Roaches; Weevils; Trash Can Repellent; Flea and Mosquito Repellent; Moths

Cleaning with Herbs   105

Household Cleaner Recipes; All-purpose Cleanser; Carpet and Upholstery Deodorizer; Wood Cleaning Polish; Room Freshener Jelly

Bath and Boudoir   109

Bronwen's Bath Tub Fizzies; Multipurpose Bath Milk; Personal Empowerment Bath and Shower Soap; Worry-Free Garden Shampoo; After Shampoo Rinse; Herbal Talcum Powder; Love and Romance Lingerie and Linen Sachet; Dryer Sachet

Herbal Beauty   119

Lemon Balm Makeup Remover; Peel-Off Mask; Moisturizing Mask; Lemon Balm Toner; Herbal Moisturizer; Dandelion Skin Bleach; Peppermint Lip Gloss; Miracle Cure for Dry, Rough Feet

Herbal Hygiene and First Aid   125

Aunt Henny's Lip Balm; Powdered Toothpaste; Herbal Mouthwash; Upset Stomach Tea; Indigestion and Heartburn Tea; Simple Cough Syrup; Sunburn Soother; Quick Herbal First Aid Fixes

Culinary Treasures   131

Herbal Vinegars; Grandma Sadie's All-purpose Seasoning Mix; Rose Geranium Jelly; Herbal Shortbread Cookies; Lavender Thirst Quencher; Quick Culinary Herbal Tricks

Herbs in the Magical Realm   137

Who's Herb? (And Why's He Talking to Me?); Magical Herb Lamps; Herbal Beeswax Candles; Quick Wish Spell; Magical Herb Beads; Herbal Paper; Basic Incense Cones; Herbal Altar Pentacle; Absinthe Liqueur; Magical Herb Wines; Basic Wine Recipe

Afterword   155

Appendix A: Resource Guide to Mail Order Seeds and Plants   157

Appendix B: Monthly Gardening Checklist   158

Appendix C: Floriography   160

Appendix D: Magical Uses of Herbs, Plants, and Flowers   164

Appendix E: Planetary Rulership   167

Appendix F: Elemental Rulership   169

Appendix G: Magical Uses of Stones   171

Bibliography   174

Index   176

Preface

I LIKE HERBS. We've had an ongoing friendship for over forty years and, unlike many of my human acquaintances, they've never let me down. Herbs first came into my life when I was less than a week old. A basket of freshly picked mint at my feet, I cooed in the stroller while Mama tended her flowerbeds. It was my first introduction to herbs, green life, and, of course, the enticing world of aroma. Today, I never smell mint without thinking of Mama, the tall glasses of Southern iced tea she served back home, or the magical remedy that kept us congestion-free in winter.

Over the years, I've become friends with a good many herbs: a sprig of oregano from the neighbor up the road; a tiny rosemary plant emancipated by the town historian. Basil, sage, lavender, and catnip came into my life, too, and, before long, we developed a loving relationship with each other—a free, easygoing friendship that greened both my thumbs and my spiritual garden.

Part of the beauty of this relationship is that herbs are an undemanding sort. Continuous human attention, though appreciated, isn't absolutely necessary to their existence.

Unlike their more cultured siblings, herbs don't care whether you pay them any attention or not. Leave them home alone for a weekend, and they'll be just as lush when you get back as they were when you left. They don't care whether you talk or sing to them—it doesn't make any difference in their growth. Fact is, they just don't need that sort of thing to survive. All they care about are the bare essentials that Mother Nature provides: a few drops of rain, the warmth of the Sun, and, of course, an inch or two of dirt. That's all they need to take hold in the Earth with a strength befitting the mightiest warrior.

If herbs are that self-sufficient, though, of what use could we possibly be to them? Why would they even bother with our friendship? It's because we bring them one important benefit that Mother Nature cannot: Our gift to the herb world is one of basic guidance.

Fact is, herbs need a sense of direction. They're an independent sort with minds of their own and wild, free spirits. With no supervision, they sprout where they want and blossom where they will. Manners mean nothing to them. They have no qualms about invading the privacy of your vegetable garden or plotting a powerful takeover in your flower bed. Their roots happily race through the Earth with an energy level that rivals that of the unruliest child. Simply put, herbs have an attitude. They can't help it. Herbs are common weed plants.

Attitude or not, these manner-deficient little friends can bring us more relaxation than a session with a massage therapist, more energy than a pound of chocolate, and lift our spirits higher than the most prescribed mood-elevator on the medical market. Herbs—regardless of their behavioral problems—are natural aromatherapists. Think I'm kidding? Just run your fingers through a bed of herbs. Inhale the breeze that stirs and note the changes in your mood and personal energy. Without even trying, herbs open a portal to another plane and grant us entrance to a place where we can escape from the rat race of life. A place to contemplate the sacred. A place conducive to the rejuvenation of mind and spirit. And they do it all by inadvertently scenting the world around them.

Herbs also provide one of the most potent magical tools known to humankind. To a large degree, the power of herbs stems from their strong, uncivilized, independent nature. When we harness that sort of wild, unregimented energy for magic, two important things happen. First, this raw energy acts as a catalyst for our spells and gives them the impetus necessary to soar directly into the Cosmos and hit their mark. Second, and just as powerful, is that as spellcasters we automatically receive any residual herbal energies. They boost our personal power, increase our magical abilities, and—because of their connection to the Earth—ground us so we're able to carry out any mundane action necessary to complete the magic at hand.

All that having been said, the most important reason to let herbs into our lives is because they provide a direct link between the Earth and the Cosmic Plane. By participating fully in their life cycles, we gain a clearer understanding of the natural order of the physical world in conjunction with the workings of the Universe. That understanding holds the key to information about our existence and the two worlds we must live in to survive. What's more, it brings answers that we thought did not exist. Answers that were right under our noses all the time. Answers we'd have found long ago if we'd just taken the time to dig in the dirt!

Acknowledgments

BOOKS AND GARDENS HAVE MANY things in common. First, ideas—like seeds—push through the surface. They sprout. They take shape. They form roots and take hold. We watch and wait, willing them to grow.

They don't. So, aggravated and frustrated, we look the other way. And just at that moment, we realize that they've not only grown, but they've taken on a life of their own. A life so verdant, so lush, and so exciting, that they've become complete right before our very eyes. Such was the case with this book.

The most important ground that books and gardens share, though, is that they both need help from outside sources. A suggestion here . . . a tip there. Knowledge from those who have been there, done that, and have lived to recount the experience. Advice that eases the growth process and prevents us from making the same mistakes. Such, too, was the case with this book.

For that reason, I'd like to thank the following folks for their roles in greening this project and bringing it into full bloom.

To my incredible husband, Mark, whose love for me consistently greens my heart and soul, and whose infallible patience, understanding, and support allows me to bud, blossom, and thrive.

To Donna Sharley, for the use of her grandmother's all-purpose seasoning mix, and for delivering hugs and advice when I needed them most; to her husband, Fred Sharley, who treated me with as much TLC as he did his roses and dirt birds; and to her son, Terry Prince, who never failed to bolster my ego and make me laugh when I didn't think I could.

To InaRae Ussack, for the gracious use of her garden blessing ritual, and for her continuous support and friendship over the years.

To Bronwen Green, who not only spent hours working up the perfect bathtub fizzie recipe, but allowed me to use it in this book.

To Patricia Telesco, for initially introducing me to this business, for her friendship, and for the generous offer of her stone charging instructions and paper-making recipe.

To Sirona Knight, Karri Allrich, Jami Shoemaker, Patricia Heller, and Sandi Liss, for their many kindnesses, for words of encouragement, and for their constant love and laughter.

To Lisa Novak, who brought this book to life with her fabulous cover design; to Karin Simoneau, who worked tirelessly to make me look good in print; and to Nancy Mostad, Acquisitions Goddess Extraordinaire, without whom I could not fly.

And finally, to you, the reader. By picking up this book and applying its ideas, you've taken the first step toward greening your thumbs, your hearts, and tending the most important garden of all—the spiritual garden; that garden which encompasses each step you walk along the personal path.

Mother Nature's Playground

PART ONE

Planning, Locating, and Preparing

THE MOST IMPORTANT PART OF herb gardening is not the actual planting—it's the decision to dig in the Earth, get your hands dirty, and let the Creator or Creatrix work through you. It's the decision to become Mother Nature's birthing coach, Her nursemaid and nanny. The decision to nurture Her seedlings straight through to blossoming adulthood. Once you've made those commitments, herb gardening is a snap. All that's left is the fun stuff: planning, planting, and harvesting.

Initializing the Magic

I like to plan my garden early—about three months before the actual planting time. This gives me time to get organized, work on planting arrangements, and order seeds. It also allows the seedlings I start indoors plenty of time to mature before I transplant them outside.

Since organization is crucial to good planning, you'll need to gather a few supplies. The essentials are listed on the following page. Feel free to add to this list as you see fit. After all, garden planning is a magical event, and anything that makes your life easier will help your magic to flow more smoothly.

LOOSE LEAF BINDER: Fill the binder with notebook paper, quarter-inch graph paper, and add some dividers if you like. Use it now to hold idea notes, symbolic shape and theme possibilities, and plant lists. Later, you can use it to keep track of planting and growth records, fertilizing notes, and related magical data.

MANILA FOLDERS: Use these to hold the brochures providing planting instructions that often accompany mail order plants and seeds. If you like, use the folders to keep track of your gardening receipts, too.

SEED AND PLANT CATALOGUES: Thumb through these to see what's available to you and what grows well in your area. (For hot and cold weather plant advice, also check out the charts at the end of this chapter.) Save time by starting a page for each company that interests you. List the company's address and phone number, then jot down the herbs they supply. Do it now, and later you won't have to tear up the house looking for information on the herbs you can't live without.

COLORED PENCILS: These are great for marking different plant varieties on garden design graphs. They also come in handy for plotting placement arrangements of short, medium, and tall plants.

CALENDAR: Find one that accurately reports monthly Moon phases. Knowing the Moon phases is essential for successfully planting bulbs, root crops, and above-ground plants. Because planetary movement can affect the Moon's garden-related power, a calendar that also lists the Moon signs is a good bet.

SMALL FILE BOX WITH INDEX CARDS: Knowing which plants have done well for me and which plants haven't is handy information to have at my fingertips. For this reason, I like to make an index card for every plant or package of seeds I buy. To do this, just mark the date of purchase in one corner of the card and the name of the store where you bought the plant in the other. Write the name of the plant on the top line, then jot down any related care requirements, gardening victories, or failures below. If you can find a picture of the plant, cut it out and glue it to the back. Keep the cards in alphabetical order and update them frequently. Keep a card labeled "Disaster" at the back of the box, and toss any "failure cards" behind it.

Magical Garden Themes

Once you've gotten organized, take a few moments to think about the type of garden you'd like to plant. Are you interested in herbal gardening solely for culinary or medicinal purposes, or are you more interested in magical property value? Perhaps you want to honor a particular deity, or use the gardening process itself for creative spellcasting. You don't have to pick just one idea or theme. If you're interested in all of the above and have enough space, consider planting several small thematical gardens in close proximity to one another. If that's not an option, you can always create an all-purpose garden by providing sections for individual purpose themes.

Garden themes benefit both the magical gardeners and the plants they care for. Not only does the theme direct the energy of the plants that live in the garden, it gives the mind a sense of direction, too. In short, the theme garden keeps you focused on your magical intent. It aids the concentration so profoundly that every time you see the garden, your magical purpose comes to mind. This brings power to your magic, and alerts the Universe that your spell is ongoing and infinite.

For your convenience, a small list of magical garden themes and plant suggestions follow below. If you choose to work with these suggestions, keep in mind that all the plants listed may not grow well in your climate. For further information, check the section titled Harmonizing With Your Climate in part one, or contact your local nursery. Other plant ideas can be found in the appendixes in the back of this book.

The Butterfly Garden

On a mundane level, this garden attracts butterflies. Plants included in the suggested plant list nourish these beautiful creatures throughout their metamorphosis by providing food for the caterpillar, shelter for the cocoon, and a proper diet for the butterfly that emerges. For this reason, please refrain from using any type of pesticide on these garden plants.

On a more spiritual level, butterflies represent the changes in our lives and the successes we achieve with each transition. They are the warriors of our spirits; the airborne soldiers who fight our spiritual transitional battles and protect us from any harm that lies ahead. This makes the Butterfly Garden a good choice for general protection magic.

SUGGESTED PLANTS FOR THE BUTTERFLY GARDEN: Anise, Bee Balm, Borage, Calendula, Dill, Fennel, Garlic Chives, Goldenrod, Lavender, Milkweed, Mints, Nasturtium, Parsley, Sorrel, Violet.

The Fairy Garden

If you have an affinity for fairies, elves, and the fey, this is the garden for you. The plants listed below attract these types, welcome them into your life, and invite them to take a hand in your magical work. Because the wee folk are known for their impulsive, whimsical attitudes, this garden is also great for those who need to add a little spontaneity to their lives.

The Fairy Garden is the most easily maintained of all the gardens listed. Once plants are secured in the Earth and the seeds are sown, no weeding is necessary. This allows the new residents to take part in the gardening and furbish their new homes as they please. Don't be surprised at the additional plant life that crops up in this space. The fairies have a way of knowing what you need, and will do everything in their power to see that you get it.

SUGGESTED PLANTS FOR THE FAIRY GARDEN: Borage, Chamomile, Choral Bells, Foxglove, Hollyhock, Lemon Balm, Maidenhair Fern, Pinks, Rosemary, St. John's Wort, Sunflower, Sweet Annie, Sweet Basil, Sweet Pea, Thyme, Violet, Wood Betony.

The Ritual Garden

Because growing plants are a natural grounding force, this garden makes the ideal spot for all your spellcasting and ritual work. Grown with a variety of herbs, it's also magically convenient. Working on a protection spell? Just pluck the herbs of your choice and use them right on the spot. For extra convenience—and magical focus—plant it in a circle and add a tree stump or large flat rock to the center for an altar. *Note:* To wrap all your magical work in "blessed be's," add a few bee-attracting plants, such as bee balm or dill.

Suggested Plants for the Ritual Garden: Apple Mint, Bergamot, Catnip, Chamomile, Lavender, Lemon Balm, Mugwort, Peppermint, Rosemary, Rue, Spearmint, Thyme, Verbena, Wormwood, Yarrow.

The Spell Garden

The Spell Garden is unique in that it uses floriography—the language of herbs and flowers—to carry a specific message to the Universe that is ongoing and infinite. For example, a strained relationship with your mother might be eased by planting a bed of goldenrod (encouragement), basil (affection), wood sorrel (maternal love), bee balm (compassion), and bay laurel (success). This tells the Universe that you wish to encourage an affectionate, compassionate, successful relationship with your mother, and that you intend for the Universe to follow suit. (For other magical message ideas or more information on floriography, see the Who's Herb? section in part two, and appendix C.)

The Meditation Garden

This garden is for everyone who needs to take some time off, relax, and regroup. Position a chair or bench in the center—you'll need a place to sit comfortably— then plant the garden around it. Use herbs that have a heady aroma. Their fragrance will help transport you to another plane—a place conducive to personal transformation, wisdom, and relaxation.

Suggested Plants for the Meditation Garden: Bay, Calendula, Chamomile, Comfrey, Dandelion, Flax, Hops, Irises, Lavender, Lemon Verbena, Mugwort, Nettle, Passion Flower, Pinks, Poppies, Roses, St. John's Wort, Scented Geraniums, Skullcap, Spearmint, Sunflower, Sweet Peas, Thyme.

The Medicine Wheel Garden

If your main focus is health and healing, the Medicine Wheel Garden is for you. Designed around the lesson, vision, and quest paths of the Native Americans, this garden is divided into four sections—representing north, east, south, and west—and circled by the moons of the year. Plant it with healing herbs for the physical body. Symptoms of the mind and spirit will ease, too.

SUGGESTED PLANTS FOR THE MEDICINE WHEEL GARDEN: Aloe Vera, Baby's Breath, Cayenne Pepper, Chamomile, Echinacea, Horehound, Lavender, Lemon Balm, Mugwort, Peppermint, Plantain, Sage, Spearmint, Thyme.

The Moon Garden

Women seem to love this garden because it invokes the feminine energy of the Goddess and Moon. Plant it with herbs that mirror your emotional needs, the transitions in your life, and the turning points in your spirituality. Plant a willow tree in the center, or place a Goddess statue or fountain there. Use it to meditate, gain insight, and perform Moon rituals. It's also the perfect place for divinatory and wish magic.

SUGGESTED PLANTS FOR THE MOON GARDEN: Daisies, Evening Primrose, Forget-me-nots, Horehound, Lavender, Lamb's Ears, Moon Flower, Mugwort, Narcissus, Rosemary, Southernwood, Sweet Cicely, Thyme, Wisteria, Yarrow.

The Sun/Moon Garden

For those striving toward perfect balance, the Sun/Moon Garden is a good bet. It radiates both the masculine and feminine energies of the Lord and Lady, and imparts harmony to all who gather there. This makes it the perfect spot for performing magical efforts that involve love, friendship, family, home, and prosperity. *Note:* For a smooth blend of the male/female energies, plant the Sun/Moon division lines with irises.

SUGGESTED PLANTS FOR THE SUN/MOON GARDEN: Black-eyed Susans, Chamomile, Daylilies, Daffodils, Daisies, Evening Primrose, Foxglove, Horehound, Irises, Lavender, Lemon Balm, Lemon Thyme, Lemon Verbena, May Apple, Mugwort, Sunflower, Yarrow.

The Culinary Garden

Although designed to delight the cook in your family, the Culinary Garden can also double as a magical one. This is because culinary herbs contain potent magic and are just as effective in the Cosmos as they are in the kitchen. Remember, too, that food presents its own kind of magic. Use a touch of cinnamon to rekindle love, a pinch of sage to impart wisdom, or a bit of spearmint to soothe a raging temper. Go on. Tickle the Cosmic Palate. What happens may amaze you.

SUGGESTED PLANTS FOR THE CULINARY GARDEN: Basil, Bay, Borage, Chamomile, Chives, Dill, Marjoram, Nasturtium, Oregano, Parsley, Peppermint, Rosemary, Sage, Sorrel, Spearmint, Tarragon, Thyme.

Shapes, Symbolism, and Magical Portents

Another planning stage consideration is the shape your planting area should take. Will a standard rectangular version suit your purposes, or would another shape mirror your needs better? I like to use symbolic shapes for magical gardens because they illustrate the garden's purpose to the Universe and reinforce that intent within the unconscious and subconscious minds. For example, I once grew a heart-shaped bed of radishes as a healing spell for a friend with a broken heart. Another time, I planted pots of pansies, forget-me-nots, spikenard, and lavender, arranged them in a circle, and used their magic for a relative experiencing memory loss. The results were phenomenal. If these ideas appeal to you, jot down any appropriate shapes and pick one that best conveys your magical message. For your convenience, a few easily managed garden shape or symbol ideas are listed below.

Circle

The circle is a feminine shape that represents continuity and continual growth for the good of all. It also provides good symbolism for the birth/death/rebirth cycle.

Crescent

Use this shape to call upon the growth energy of the waxing moon. It also works well for general magic or efforts involving psychic power or divination.

Diamond

Because of its perfect symmetry, the diamond vibrates toward harmony. This makes it an excellent shape for meditation gardens or those used for culinary purposes. As this shape also vibrates toward the solidity of Earth, it's a good bet for magical gardens involving prosperity and abundance, and issues of the family, home, and hearth.

Element Wheel

This garden is divided into four equal portions by an *X* in the center. Do some research and use plants that correspond to each Element in the appropriate sections. Plant the center with those plants ruled by Akasha (spirit) if you like.

Moon Phases

This garden consists of a central circle with a crescent pointing outward on either side. Use it to honor the Maiden, Mother, and Crone, or to invoke the powers of the Moon.

Pentagram

Called the Witches' Garden for obvious reasons, this layout is a five-pointed star encompassed by a circle. Because this is an all-protecting, omnimagical symbol, ideas for specific magical efforts are endless. For instance, you might dedicate it to the Elements by planting blooming plants in the colors and sections appropriate to Akasha, Air, Fire, Water, and Earth, and placing God or Goddess symbols or plants in the center. Want a multipurpose magical garden? Use each section for a different magical intent. With this shape, your only limitation is the size of your imagination.

Rectangle

Most gardens are planted in this shape for several reasons. For one thing, it's easy to work with and accommodates a wide assortment of plants. But magically speaking, there's another reason. The rectangle has tremendous holding power and acts as a magical binder. It works well for any magical garden, but especially for efforts involving protection, health and healing, or warding off harm. To safeguard your house or family members, plant your herb garden in rectangular beds all around your home. It will act as a Cosmic security guard.

Square

Since the square contains sides of equal length, a garden of this shape vibrates toward balance. As it provides the perfect symbol for solid, dependable, organized efforts, it can be used to increase the focus and concentration of any magical theme. This shape can also be divided equally into four parts and planted with appropriate herbs to symbolize the Elements. If you like, plant a tree or bush in the center to represent Akasha.

Triangle

Because this figure represents the creative force within, it works well for gardens planted to invoke the properties of imagination, inspiration, good fortune, and magical mastery. Plant it in three sections to invoke the powers of the Triple Goddess or Triple God.

Wheel

The wheel is a circle divided into eight equal sections or spokes. Use it to represent the Wheel of the Year, planting different herbs in each section. Place symbols of the God and Goddess—stones, seashells, a bird bath filled with water, and so on—in the center to represent the balance of male and female and the perfect harmony of the seasons.

Harmonizing with Your Climate

One of the most valuable keys to successful gardening is learning to plant in harmony with your local climate. There's a sound reason for this. The fact is, no matter how badly you may want to grow certain plants, some of them just don't thrive outside of their native habitats. Because of this, it's best to determine which type of climate you live in, then plan to garden with plants that do well there.

How do you know which plants will be happy in your area? Zoning maps (maps of the country in which you live that are divided into numbered sections, or zones) can help with this. Most seed and plant catalogues (and the backs of seed packets) are clearly marked with zoning information. All you have to do is match up your zone number to the appropriate seeds or plants.

Another way to ensure success is to pay a visit to the botanical gardens in your area. Talk to the horticulturists or groundskeepers there. In lieu of that, check out the gardens in your neighborhood. Don't be afraid to knock on some doors if you have questions. Gardening enthusiasts are always happy to talk about their plants and gardening skills, and are delighted to have an opportunity to pat themselves on the back. Who knows? You may just wind up with a wealth of free gardening advice, starts of plants that you'd normally have to order, and a new friend—all because you summoned the courage to rap upon some unknown door!

In the meantime, though, take a look at the climate charts below. Although they're not by any means complete, the plants listed will help you get started.

Cold Climate Herbs

If temperatures in your area frequently drop below 10 degrees Fahrenheit, try these herbs in your magical garden. Although they grow well in warmer climates, they have a great tolerance for cold weather.

Angelica, Anise, Barberry, Bearberry, Bee Balm, Betony, Borage, Burdock, Caraway, Catmint, Chamomile, Chervil, Chicory, Chives, Elecampane, Garlic, Goldenrod, Hops, Horseradish, Horsetail, Hyssop, Indigo, Lady's Bedstraw, Life Everlasting, Nasturtium, Nettle, Purple Coneflower, Plantain, Red Clover, Roses, Saffron, Sweet Cicely, Sweet Woodruff, Tansy, Tarragon, Valerian, Vervain, Wormwood, Yarrow

Warm Climate Herbs

If you live in an area where temperatures never drop below 10 Fahrenheit, try the herbs listed below as well as those listed on the previous page.

Agrimony, Basil, Bay, Balendula, Cayenne Pepper, Coriander, Eucalyptus, Fennel, Fenugreek, Feverfew, Geranium, Horehound, Lavender, Lemongrass, Lemon Verbena, Marjoram, Mint Oregano, Orris, Parsley, Passionflower, Pennyroyal, Rosemary, Rue, Safflower, Sage, Santolina, Southernwood, Thyme, Violet, Witch Hazel

Dry Climate Herbs

Try plants from this list if you live in a dry, arid area that seldom sees rainfall.

Burdock, Catnip, Chicory, Costmary, Elecampane, Goldenrod, Hyssop, Marjoram, Oregano, Pennyroyal, Rue, Santolina, Winter Savory, Southernwood, Thyme, Wormwood

Tropical/Rainy Climate Herbs

These plants grow well in very humid areas, or those where rainfall is plentiful.

Azaleas, Basil, Catnip, Cinquefoil, Coral Bells, Daisy, Delphinium, Echinacea, Evening Primrose, Fern, Foxglove, Geranium, Lady's Mantle, Lavender, Mallow, Parsley, Peony, Rosemary, Sage, Thyme, Verbena, Yarrow

Herbs for Shady Areas

Even though this herb list really has nothing to do with climate, it's been added here to help you plan for gardening areas that seldom receive full sun.

Agrimony, Angelica, Bay, Bee Balm, Lemon Balm, Betony, Catnip, Chamomile, Chervil, Comfrey, Coriander, Costmary, Feverfew, Horsetail, Hyssop, Lovage, Mint, Parsley, Pennyroyal, Plantain, Sweet Cicely, Sweet Woodruff, Tansy, Tarragon, Thyme, Valerian, Violet, Wormwood

Herbs Need Friends, Too

While working with your climate certainly does wonders for your garden, planting certain herbs beside each other can make a remarkable difference, too. This is because herbs, like people, have friends. When put into an environment with the plants they enjoy, herbs grow taller, bushier, and more luxurious. Their overall health improves. Because they are happy, they thrive.

Partial lists of companion plants follow below. For more information on companion planting, talk to the folks at your local library or garden center.

BASIL: Salad burnet, Chives, Oregano.

CHIVES: Comfrey, Lavender, Roses.

CILANTRO: Basil, Lemon Balm, Oregano.

LEMON BALM: Fennel, Parsley.

MARJORAM: Bee Balm, Oregano, Thyme.

Sizing the Magic

Once you've thought about plants and figured out the type and shape of the garden you want, give a little thought to your herbal space needs. How many plant varieties do you intend to grow? Is the garden for personal use, or do your plans include supplying several people with herbs? Keep your garden type and shape selections in mind as you think about this. A culinary garden confined to a small area might be more effective and convenient than a large one. If you want to grow plants for their magical properties, though, you may need more space to accommodate a greater variety of herbs.

I made a big sizing mistake with my first herb garden. It never occurred to me that herbs needed lots of space to grow and spread out. I planted them just like flowers, and the result was disastrous. The hardier plants eradicated the more delicate ones. Even worse, some of the more unruly varieties intermingled with the others and interchanged scents. When all was said and done, I couldn't tell the orange mint from the pennyroyal. Not knowing which was which, the plants were worthless to me—both magically and mundanely.

For this reason, plan your garden size very carefully. I find quarter-inch graph paper helpful for this. First, decide how many plant varieties you want to grow. Then, using one square per foot, figure your garden size. Allow at least one foot between plants. This will give your herbs all the spreading room they need, and you won't have to worry about your catnip smelling like lemon balm.

When plotting garden size, don't forget to consider how much room you'll need for walking, weeding, and general tending. Two to three feet between each row or section is a good bet. If you're thinking of adding a park bench, bird bath, or other item, figure its dimensions, then add an extra two to three feet of space to each side. There's nothing more aggravating than planting a beautiful garden, only to discover that you have no way to nurture it, enjoy it, or harvest the fruits of your labor.

One last thing. As a magical practitioner, you'll probably want the fairies, elves, gnomes, and other Earth Spirits to help you with your garden. The best way to enlist their aid is to give them a personal spot in the garden. If this appeals to you, add an extra foot or two somewhere in your completed plans. Where you add it doesn't matter; Earth Spirits are happy in any location. If you're worried about space, even a small corner will do. It's only important that you give them their space willingly. Take it from someone who knows: If you take care of the Earth Spirits, they'll take care of you and every magical effort you perform. It's the most important space you can plot in your plans.

Choosing an Outdoor Gardening Spot

One of the most important factors in the gardening process is deciding where to plant. While hilltop gardens might appeal to your artistic nature—and can work in some cases—they usually don't provide an atmosphere suitable for healthy, thriving plants. This is because strong winds and thunderstorms can cause soil erosion, and the last thing you want is for your precious seeds and plants to wash downhill in a river of muddy slush.

Valleys have their drawbacks, too. For one thing, water tends to settle in low spots. This can cause root and seed rot. More important, though, stagnant water provides an excellent breeding ground for mosquitoes and all sorts of other flesh-stinging critters. Even if some of your plants manage to temporarily survive the swamp, you may not be able to get close enough to them for comfortable tending.

Instead, look for a flat, level area. Drainage won't be a problem, and neither will mosquitoes. Try to avoid rocky places or locations where tree roots might interfere with tilling and soil preparation. It's also a good idea to choose a spot that gets at least four hours of sunshine a day. Spend some time in the spot to get a handle on the times of day that provide sun and shade. This information is indispensable for planning plant varieties and placement.

If you're not fortunate enough to have a flat outdoor space, choose a sloping spot rather than a hilltop or valley. Set plants out instead of sowing seeds. Because most plants have solid root formations, they're less likely to wash downhill. To guarantee that plants will stay where you put them, consider planting across the slope rather than straight up and down. This type of planting prevents soil erosion and keeps the valley below swamp-free.

When you find a spot that appeals to you, take a few minutes to go through the checklist below. If something doesn't check out, you'll have an opportunity to rethink your plans before you dig.

- Is the area close to your home? This is important for two reasons. First, you're more likely to weed, fertilize, and prune if it doesn't mean a half-hour hike every day. You'll also spend more time there if you only have to step outside to enjoy its fragrant beauty.

- Is the space large enough to accommodate your plans? If you're not sure, get out the tape measure. Taking a few measurements will save time and disappointment later.

- Are there adequate faucet hookups and water spigots in close proximity? Convenience is a priority here. Hauling buckets of water on a daily basis gets old quickly. As a result, you may not give the garden the attention it needs.

Gardening Permission Ritual

Once you've found the ideal gardening spot, it's a good idea to ask the resident Earth Spirits for permission to use it. Take a few minutes and sit in the center of the area. Dig your fingers into the soil and experience the rich dampness of the earth. Close your eyes and watch as your fingers become root systems and travel happily beneath the surface. See the lush foliage sprout from your body. Watch it blossom and bear fruit. Savor the breeze, the sunshine, and the moisture in the air.

When you become fully attuned to the plant world, talk to the Earth Spirits. Let them know what you want to do. Invoke Them by saying something like:

Earth Spirits of this place, come near
I've something to say that I want You to hear
I ask for this space for a garden today
To till it, and grow it, and tend it my way
To carefully nurture each plant that I grow
To love, cherish, and care for this place as my own
I ask Your permission, O Spirits of Earth
I wait for Your answer in love, light, and mirth

Then wait for an answer or signal of approval. This could be a word that echoes through your brain, a falling leaf, a sudden gust of wind, or something much more subtle. Once approval is given, offer the Earth Spirits a bit of yourself in return—a strand of hair, a fingernail clipping, or a drop of saliva works well—and bury it in the soil. This offering not only creates a personal bond with the garden spot, but assures the resident spirits that you will tend to the area's personal needs with the same care you give to your own.

Once you have permission to use the spot, it's a good idea to start a compost heap. This serves several purposes. For one thing, compost benefits all but the wettest garden areas. It enriches the soil and provides nutrients that plants can absorb and digest easily. It's also an excellent way to recycle your table scraps, grass clippings, dead leaves, and other things you'd normally leave for the garbage truck. But most importantly, preparing compost is a great way to ensure the continued blessings of the Earth Spirits. It lets them know you're serious, and that while the area is under your care, you'll do everything you can to improve its condition.

Compost Recipe

Although compost isn't hard to make, it does take several months to cure properly. Start your compost heap now, and you won't have to wait to use it in your garden later—you'll have plenty of useable organic matter when you need it. All that's necessary is a three to four foot area outside.

Layer One

Place two to three inches of straw, twigs, or sawdust in the compost area. (You can get sawdust free of charge from the local lumber yard. In lieu of that, try your local cabinet maker.) These materials provide good drainage, proper aeration, and keep your compost from molding.

Layer Two

Pile three to six inches of grass clippings, dead leaves, or kitchen scraps on top of the drainage material. Eggshells, vegetable and fruit peelings and cores, used coffee grounds and tea leaves, stale bread, and other nonmeat perishables are good candidates for compost.

Layer Three

Add two to three inches of animal manure (horse stables, auction barns, chicken and dairy farms, and circus managers will let you have this for the taking) or commercial fertilizer.

Layer Four

Add an inch or two of topsoil.

Continue to layer the materials until the pile is about four feet high. If you live in a very dry area, sprinkle the mixture with water every few days. Turn and mix the compost after the first three weeks, then once each week thereafter. It's ready to use when the mixture is brown and crumbles easily.

Choosing an Indoor Gardening Location

You may not be lucky enough to have a plot of ground outside just waiting around for you to plant something on it. That doesn't mean you can't have an herb garden, though. All you need is a sunny window or an empty corner in your home. With a little extra lighting, even a spot under the stairs will do.

I like to use a southern exposure for herbal window gardening. This is because southern light isn't as harsh as that provided by the east and west, and you don't have to worry about the drafty chill that accompanies a north window in the winter. If you don't have a south window, though, all is not lost. Pick the sunniest window in your house. Then, instead of placing your garden pots on a windowsill, prepare a spot on the floor below it. This will help to shield your plants from the damage of harsh rays or icy glass.

If you don't have any windows—or enough room for a garden in a windowed area—choose a spot that's accessible and fairly draft-free. (Be sure it's a place you'll notice every day. While herbs don't need much attention to thrive outside, they'll wither away to nothing if you forget to water them indoors.)

You can always install some fluorescent lights above the gardening area. They're very inexpensive and will provide all the light you need. (For further information about indoor gardening, please see the Learning, Turning, and Discerning section.)

Home Spirit Help Ritual

Use this ritual for starting seeds or total indoor gardening. While you may not have to gain permission to garden in your own home, it's a good idea to ask your Home Spirit to help you look after the garden spot. This not only gives the Spirit something to do and keeps It out of mischief, it provides a great deal of protection for the plants you'll grow there.

All you need for this ritual is a supply of white seven-day candles and some heartfelt enthusiasm. Take the candle to your indoor gardening area and light it. Then warmly invoke your Home Spirit and Its help by saying something like:

> *Spirit of the Home, come near*
> *And this plea for help, please hear*
> *Watch over this spot with love and care*
> *Bring to it Your style and flair*
> *Protect it with Your will and might*
> *So what I plant grows lush and bright*
> *Bring plants to blossom, then to seed*
> *Tend their magic till it's freed*
> *And as a token gift for all You do*
> *I'll keep this candle lit for You*

The only catch to this little ritual is that you must never let the candle burn out. (If you do, the Home Spirit will think that Its services are no longer necessary, and that you don't love It anymore.) This really isn't the problem it may seem. Just light another seven-day candle before the lit one burns out. Fortunately, these candles are very inexpensive and easily accessible. You can usually find them at the supermarket.

Starting Seedlings Indoors

Planting seeds outdoors is a precarious venture. You can water, weed, and fertilize. You can beg and plead. But sometimes, no matter what you do, they just refuse to sprout. In the final analysis, all you're left with is a rich plot of ground and a bad attitude. This doesn't have to happen to you. All you need is some basic knowledge and a spot indoors to start your seeds.

Seeds fail miserably outdoors for a number of reasons: Sometimes birds eat the seeds before they can germinate; sometimes a late frost is the culprit; most of the time, though, seeds meet their demise because certain conditions in the soil—conditions caused by resident bugs and parasites—just aren't favorable for effective germination.

The fact is, a seed is much like a human fetus. It needs proper nourishment. It needs protection from the elements. It needs time to grow in the warmth of the mother's belly. Unlike the human fetus, though, a seed has no immune system of its own and can't "borrow" one from the mother. It has no way to ward off disease or defend itself against possible damage. This means that you—the gardener—have to provide it with a special environment. An environment conducive to its healthy birth and continuing growth.

Blessing the Seeds

One of the best ways to create a proper environment for your seeds is to bless them with a protective spell. I like to do this about eight to ten weeks before I plant the garden. In my area, this falls close to Imbolc, so I incorporate the spell into my Imbolc ritual. Since climate varies place to place, though, you might find it more convenient to bless your seeds during a different Sabbat, or set aside some other time to work this spell. The materials you will need for this ritual are as follows:

> Seed packets
> Basket
> Light incense
> Green candle
> Dish of water

Gather the materials and go to a spot where you won't be disturbed. Place the seed packets next to the basket, and light the candle and the incense. Hold a packet and pass it through the incense smoke. Say something like:

> *I give you Air*
> *Breathe deep and long*
> *May winds and breezes*
> *Make you strong*

Pass the seed packet through the candle flame and say something like:

> *I give you Fire*
> *Feel the heat of Sun*
> *Bask in its warmth*
> *'Til harvest comes*

Sprinkle the packet with a few drops of water. Say something like:

> *I give you Water*
> *Drink deep the rain*
> *To quench your thirst*
> *And growing pains*

Then hold the packet to your breast and say:

I give you Earth
Sink well your roots
To grab its wealth
And bring green shoots

Visualize the seeds germinating, sprouting, and growing into a thriving, lush green plant. Say something like:

I see you grow
And as I do
New life stirs inside of you
Your roots grow deep
In dampened soil
Your foliage sprouts in green so royal
Until mature plants
You become
By Air, Earth, Rain, and shining Sun

Repeat this process with every seed variety, then put the seed packets in the basket and leave them there until the candle burns down.

Sterilizing the Soil

Another way to provide the perfect growing environment for seeds is to start them in a sterile, soilless potting mixture—you'll want to do this about ten weeks before you plant the garden. Sterile? Soilless? You bet. While particular fungi, bacteria, and parasites make garden soil rich and are excellent for semimature plants, they mean certain death to seedlings. Something as fragile and delicate as a seed just isn't able to handle the vigorous nature of these microscopic organisms. It needs time to rest, grow, and adjust. Placing seeds in the same area with these busy microbes is tantamount to turning the stereo on full blast in your baby's nursery. It not only makes the seedling cranky, but messes with its growth patterns and central nervous system. You usually wind up with a neurotic, spindly plant with root rot, or no plant at all.

Most commercial soilless potting mixes are a blend of peat moss, perlite, and vermiculite. They are inexpensive and readily available at nurseries, garden centers, discount stores, and supermarkets. But what if you live out in the middle of nowhere and getting to the store is a real pain? What then? One solution is to dig up some of your garden soil and sterilize it. Just spread the soil evenly on cookie sheets, set the oven for 180 degrees, and let it bake for three or four hours. Once every hour, chant something like:

> *Microscopic things that harm*
> *Leave now as this soil gets warm*
> *As this Earth is cleansed by Fire*
> *It takes the form that I desire*

When the soil cools, you have a harm-free ready-to-use potting mix for your precious seeds. Best of all, it didn't cost a cent!

Cleansing Pots and Containers

Once you have a sterile potting medium, find some cell-packs (a potting flat divided into tiny compartments) or gather an assortment of small pots with drainage holes in the bottom.

Whether the pots are plastic or clay doesn't matter. It only matters that you wash them well with hot soapy water—even if you just brought them home from the store. Why? First, it's common practice to store gardening containers with pesticides, herbicides, and other chemicals. A spillage of that nature might impede seedling growth or prevent it altogether.

Another reason is that there's no way to tell exactly where the containers originally came from or what sort of environmental hazards they were exposed to. For example, you wouldn't want to plant the seeds only to discover that your gardening containers were infested with some type of exotic mite—especially after you went to all the trouble to make sure your potting mix was sterile. The idea is to destroy anything that might impede the growth process of your seeds.

The key to sterilizing pots is to wash and rinse them in very hot water. Toss clay pots right into the dishwasher if you like. Plastic pots can be washed in the dishwasher, too, if you place them on the top rack. If you prefer to wash your pots by hand, please use rubber gloves to protect your hands. It will take a long time for your thumbs to grow green if they're covered with blisters!

As you wash the pots, chant something like:

Fire and Water, wash these clean
Of harmful stuff that isn't seen
And when You're done, please sterilize
So little seeds will sprout and rise

More Seed Planting Preparations

Even though you're armed with the main ingredients for healthy seed starting—seeds, sterile potting mix, and sterilized planting containers—you're not quite ready to dig in and plant. Why? Because just like members of the human race, every seed variety is slightly different: Some varieties enjoy cold weather; some like warmth and excessive moisture; others have hard shells. Commercially harvested seeds—even those varieties indigenous to your area—can be lackluster and difficult to grow because they don't get to experience the normal cold, hot, moist, dry periods of the seasonal cycle. This means you may have to figure out what each variety needs to persuade it to germinate.

Deciding which seeds need what isn't always easy. For immediate help, read the back of the seed package. It contains valuable information such as the types of climate the plant is used to and the zones that are best suited for healthy plant growth. From this information, you can usually determine which of the methods listed below is most conducive to the best interest of your seeds.

Technique One: Adding Moisture

One way to jump-start seeds is to soak them in water prior to planting. The reasoning behind this is simple. Exposure to moisture softens the seed shell, penetrates the embryo, and tells the seed that it's time to grow. While all varieties benefit from this process, I find that method one works best on medium to large seeds. For tiny seeds, try method two.

METHOD ONE: Start by filling a small shallow baking dish (glass works best) with hot tap water. Empty the seed packet into the dish and spread the seeds out a bit. Lay your hands over the dish and chant:

> *Seeds that hold the life source in:*
> *Burst forth and grow; it's Spring again!*

Leave the seeds to soak for at least twelve hours, but no longer than twenty-four (a lengthier period of time could cause the seeds to rot). Strain out the seeds, then blot them well with several layers of paper toweling. Plant the seeds according to the package directions.

METHOD TWO: For this method, you'll need a separate plastic zipper bag (gallon size works well for each seed variety), and some paper toweling. Wet a paper towel, squeeze out the excess water, and spread the towel out on a flat surface. Using the chant listed for method one, sprinkle the seeds on one half of the towel, then fold the other half over them to cover. Insert the seeded towel into the bag, zip it shut, and mark the seed variety on the bag front. Wait a day or two, then check for sprouts by holding the bag up to a strong light. (Some seeds take longer to germinate than others, so you may want to check the bags daily.) When the seeds have sprouted, plant them in pots of sterilized soil.

Technique Two: Seed Stratification

Some seeds are used to cold climates. While in their native habitats they know exactly what to do—when to germinate, when to grow, and when to blossom. But when they wind up in warmer areas of the country, a problem often occurs. The seeds stagnate. Gardeners do everything they can think of, but it's no use. The seeds simply never come up. It's not the gardener's fault. The seeds are just confused.

Fortunately, this problem is easily rectified with something called stratification. Don't be put off by the term; it's just a fancy word. Simply put, it means tricking the seed into thinking it's back home in the cold, and that the time has come to germinate.

Stratifying seeds is easy. All you need are some sandwich-sized plastic zipper bags, a bit of sterile potting mix, and your refrigerator. First, soak the seeds as described in method one in the Adding Moisture section. Fill the bags half-full of sterile potting mix and add the seeds. Using the chant described in the Adding Moisture section, top off with another inch of mix. Zip the bag and place it in the refrigerator.

Check weekly for signs of germination. When root systems begin to form, carefully lift out the sprouts with a teaspoon and transplant them into pots.

Technique Three: Scarification

Some seeds have shells so tough that water can't penetrate them well. When this happens, moisture doesn't reach the embryo and the seed has no way to germinate. This is where scarification—a word meaning "to scar or nick"—comes in. But since everyone has a different idea of what "tough" is, how do you tell which seeds will benefit from this process? A good rule of thumb is to rub a fingernail across the seed surface. If your nail makes a dent, leave it alone. If not, prepare to scarify.

All you need for this process is a small jar with a screw-on lid, a piece of sandpaper cut to fit the inside perimeter of the jar, and some seeds. Simply line the jar with the sandpaper, add the seeds and a few drops of water, then screw on the lid. Shake the jar vigorously until abrasions on the seed coats are plainly seen. As you shake the jar, chant something like:

> *Little seeds of toughest shell*
> *Soak up the water in this well*

Because scarified seeds tend to dry out in a hurry, plant them as quickly as possible.

All this done, you're ready to plant, right? Not quite. You'll need to gather a few more things before you can actually pot the seeds: a spray bottle filled with water, some plastic wrap, a few craft sticks, and a marker with a fine tip. Set the items in front of you and bless them by saying something like:

Tools of Life's Creative Force
I bless you with my Power Source
Become now tools of magic seen
And help these seeds grow lush and green

Then fill each container with potting mix and say:

O mix so gentle and so clean
Give my seeds just what they need
To be born into this world anew
Do now what I ask of you

Write the names of your seed varieties on craft sticks, then plant the appropriate seeds. It's a good idea to plant several seeds for each herb plant you want. For example, if you're counting on three basil plants, sow four seeds in each of three pots. This ensures that at least one seed per pot will germinate. As you plant the seeds, say something like:

I plant you firmly in the ground
May healthy growth now soon abound

Push the craft sticks into their related pots, and moisten the seeds and potting mix with the spray bottle. Cover the containers with plastic wrap and set them near a sunny window or beneath some artificial lighting. Give the seeds a final blessing of encouragement by holding your hands over the pots and saying something like:

Grow deep, grow well, grow lush, grow green
Grow tall, grow short, or in-between
I hold all harm and ill at bay
Now grab new life and seize the day

The amount of time that it takes seeds to sprout varies from variety to variety, but you should see results in three to ten days. Since the plastic wrap acts as an automatic watering device, check the potting soil every other day to make sure it isn't too wet. If it's soggy, remove the wrap for a few hours to let the mix dry out a little (this prevents seed and root rot). If the mix is dry, spray it again with the water bottle. When the mix returns to the damp stage, replace the wrap and let Nature take Her course.

Protection for Sprouts and Seedlings

Sprouts, like babies, need special care when they enter our world. They need something to boost their immune systems and ward off infectious disease. Babies get it from regular vaccinations. Sprouts, however, only need a periodical sip of tea.

Although babies are prone to many childhood diseases—mumps, measles, chickenpox, and so on—sprouts and seedlings grown indoors only have to worry about one. It's a fungal disease called *damping-off,* and it's a real killer. The problem with damping-off is that you seldom see it coming. One day the sprouts are green and healthy. The next, they're wilted into a toppled, crumpled heap. And no amount of water, light, or sweet talk will bring them back.

Fortunately, preventing this assassin from invading your seedlings is easy. Just boil four cups of water and add one teaspoon of dried chamomile flowers or one bag of chamomile tea. As you add the chamomile, chant something like:

> *Fire and water, herb and air*
> *Blend to form an army rare*
> *Join your forces—be as one*
> *As I will, so be it done*

Let the mixture steep for twenty-four hours, then pour it in your plant mister. Give new sprouts a thorough spritzing as soon as they appear. As you mist, chant something like:

> *Warrior strong, ward off disease*
> *So these new sprouts can grow with ease*

Continue to mist the seedlings periodically (about once a week) until the second sets of leaves appear.

Learning, Turning, and Discerning

WAITING FOR SEEDS TO MATURE is much like waiting for a kettle to boil—it just doesn't seem to happen while you're watching. If your patience is running thin, turn your attention to another area of the gardening process—that of magical tool collection.

Tools of the Trade

Gardening—like every other form of ritual magic—requires a unique tool set. What you need depends on the type of garden you have in mind and how much money you want to spend. Unless you're planning to set up individual outdoor gardens year 'round, for example, you may not really need to buy a tiller; they're expensive, and you can probably get by with renting one once or twice a year. Other items are necessities, though. For your convenience, lists of bare essentials for indoor and outdoor gardening are listed below.

INDOOR TOOL LIST: Gardening shears or scissors, hand-held claw, hand-held shovel, watering can or pitcher, wide assortment of pots, windsock (to hang outside a nearby window).

OUTDOOR TOOL LIST: Garden rake, garden shears or scissors, garden spade, hoe, watering can (for fertilizing), water hose, windsock.

If you already have these tools locked away in a shed somewhere, don't run out and buy new ones. Whether magical gardening tools are new or used doesn't make any difference here. What does matter is that you treat them just like your other magical tools. Cleanse them, consecrate them, and store them away carefully. Give them the respect they deserve, and they will serve you with as much power as any wand or athame in your possession.

Rather than blessing garden tools individually, try consecrating them all at once. It not only takes less time, but unites the tools as a team and lets them know they need to work together for successful magic.

Tool Consecration

On a sunny day (during the period of New to Full Moon), gather the tools and take them to your garden spot. Place them in the center of the area, then tie the tools together with a length of green ribbon or yarn. Say something like:

You are a team now—I bind you as one
To complete every task that soon must be done
Work well together and lighten the load
Of birthing and tending this garden abode

Sit down and get comfortable. Then hold the tools in your lap or lay your hands on them, saying:

Tools of the Earth, Tools Who create
Become now tools who exacerbate
The magic I'll perform within
This plot of Earth that I'll soon tend

Lick your finger and rub a little saliva on the ribbon. Say:

I bless you with Water

Blow on the tools and say:

I bless you with Air

Gather a few grains of dirt from the spot (house dust will do if your gardening spot is indoors) and sprinkle it over the tools. Say:

I bless you with Earth

Expose the tools to the heat of the Sun (or an indoor lamp) for a few seconds and say:

And Sunshine fair

Kiss the tools or hug them to your body and say:

My magical tools, you've now become
As I will, so be it done

Leave the tools tied together and store them in a safe place until it's time to use them.

Marking the Outdoor Garden Area

Geometrically shaped gardens aren't difficult to mark. All you need is a tape measure, a couple of stakes, and some string to plot out perfectly straight edges. Round gardens and those with curving shapes are a different matter, but with a little practice and the following technique, you can create any shape you want in no time flat.

Place a stick or dowel in the middle of the area and push it firmly into the ground. Tie a piece of string around the stick, then, holding the string, walk away from the center until you reach the desired outside perimeter. Tie the other end of the string to a bottle of carpenter's chalk. Pull slightly against the string to tighten it, then turn the bottle upside down and walk slowly in a circular motion around the space. The chalk will leave its mark on the area, and you'll know exactly where to dig or till.

Note: If grass is a problem or you don't want to till the garden right away, fill a plastic squeeze bottle with white vinegar and use it in place of the chalk. This will kill the grass and weeds along the boundary line in a matter of days.

Turning, Tilling, and Playing in the Dirt

I've always liked to play in the dirt. There's just something very comforting about it. No matter what sort of mess creeps into your life, digging in the dirt seems to whisk it all away. It has a way of bringing instant peace of mind during even the worst kinds of trouble. It's one of the reasons so many gardeners enjoy the initial preparations as much as the actual planting.

Garden preparations also give you a chance to wake the Earth and play a major role in the creative process. This makes the time you spend working the soil perfect for increasing the magical power held in the garden spot. Some folks like to do this with chants. Others like to sing. For this reason, appropriate chants are listed below with each preparatory step. If you'd rather put them to music, try the tune of "Mary Had a Little Lamb."

Preparing the garden area isn't difficult. All it takes is a little time, a little effort, and careful adherence to the three simple steps listed below. Before you know it, you'll be doing more than just playing in the dirt. You'll be helping the Earth—and yourself—green and thrive with the magic and power of creative growth. So, untie your tools, put the ribbon in a safe place (you'll need it later), and let's get started.

Step One: Defining the Magic

It's important to firmly define the garden boundaries for two reasons. First, it keeps people from stepping on your seeds and plants. Second, a good boundary line works somewhat like the ritual Circle: It holds the magic of the garden inside and allows its power to increase on a constant basis.

The easiest way to do this is with the garden spade. Carefully following the chalk or vinegar outline, make firm, deep, swift cuts. As you work, chant or sing something like:

> *Garden spade of strength and might*
> *Cut this edge both clean and tight*
> *Keep the power well within*
> *This garden spot that I now tend*

Step Two: Waking the Magic

When the garden edge is completely cut in, use the tiller or hoe to turn the soil to a one-foot depth. Magically, it makes no difference which tool you use. Tilling just takes less time. If you choose to use a hoe, chop into the soil with quick, deep cuts that are close together. As you work, chant or sing something like:

Garden hoe/tilling machine, cut quick and deep
Wake the Earth now from Her sleep
So that plants and seeds will grow/green
Awaken Her richness, garden hoe/tilling machine

Step Three: Refining the Magic

Afterward, remove all the grass and weeds from the spot with the garden rake. (If you didn't use a tiller, a second hoeing may be necessary for thorough removal.) An appropriate chant for this task might be:

Garden rake, remove debris
Rake this spot clean as can be
Prepare this place for plants and seeds
And rake it free of useless weeds

When you're finished, pick up a handful of dirt. If it's soft and crumbles easily, you're ready to plant. If not, try the suggestions below for specific soil problems.

If garden soil clumps together, it won't drain well. This means root rot, spindly seedlings, and yellowed, anemic-looking plants. To solve this problem, work some sand or vermiculite into the soil.

Soil that neither clumps nor crumbles signifies too much sand. This means the soil won't hold water long enough to feed your plants. To rectify this problem, add some compost or other organic matter.

When the garden is ready for planting, lay any flagstones or walkways that fit your plans, then take a little time to thank the Spirits for the loan of Their property. This doesn't have to be an elaborate ritual; a few impromptu words of thanks work just as well. For your convenience, my favorite thank-you ritual follows below. Use it if you like, or work up one of your own. All that matters is that you welcome Them and give them Their due.

The Thanksgiving Ritual

Go to the garden with your windsock (bring a pole for hanging if there's not a nearby tree), four sticks of incense, a large cup of water, and the ribbon from your tool consecration. Hang the windsock just outside the garden perimeters (preferably in the east) and say:

> *Spirits of Air that blow and swirl*
> *Who create and inspire with every twirl*
> *I invite You—come into this space today*
> *So I can honor and thank You in a personal way*

Plant the incense sticks equidistantly around the garden boundary. Light the incense and say:

> *Spirits of Fire that power the Sun*
> *Flickering, burning, dancing as One*
> *I invite You—come into this space today*
> *So I can honor and thank You in a personal way*

Take the ribbon and bury it in the center of the garden. (If your garden is indoors, bury the ribbon in a flower pot.) As you cover it with soil, say:

> *Spirits of Earth that nurture and grow*
> *I bring you this ribbon of magic to sow*
> *I invite You—come into this space today*
> *So I can honor and thank You in a personal way*

Traveling clockwise, dip your fingers in the water and sprinkle the inside edges of the garden. As you asperge, say:

> *Watery Spirits, You Givers of Life*
> *Whose moisture can soothe and relieve famine's strife*
> *I invite You—come into this space today*
> *So I can honor and thank You in a personal way*

Stand in the middle of the garden and hold your arms up high in embrace. Then say something like:

Spirits of Air, Fire, Water, and Earth
I conjure You freely in love and in mirth
Please come now and play here as long as you like
Freely dance to Your rhythms in joyous delight
Take this offering of thanks for all that You do
And for the loan of this space that belonged just to You

Let the incense burn out, and pour any leftover water on the spot where you buried the ribbon.

Without a doubt, the most aggravating part of outdoor gardening is getting through the waiting period—that seemingly endless block of time between preparing the garden and planting it; that time spent waiting for the last frost of the year. Over the years, though, I've learned to put that time to good use. It provides a good time to watch the weather, work with the windsock, and check the local nurseries for healthy garden plants. Because I'm the impatient sort, it also gives me time to do the following ritual—a ritual that you'll want to perform, too, if spring isn't arriving quickly enough to suit you.

Invoke the Spring Ritual

All you need for this ritual is a spoon, a bowl, a hand spade for digging, some soil from outside (if the soil is frozen, so much the better), and a fervent desire to get on with the spring season.

Fill the bowl half full with soil and bring it indoors. If you have a fireplace, place it on the hearth. If not, set the bowl in another warm spot in your home. Any place is fine as long as the spot is a prominent one. Stir the soil with the spoon or crumble it with your hands. As you work the soil, chant something like:

Sleeping Earth, wake now—arise!
Rub the sleep from dreaming eyes
Yawn and stretch—wake up and bring
The verdant greening of the Spring

Stir the soil and do the chant every day for seven days. At the end of the week, sprinkle the soil outdoors. Say something like:

> Earth, take notice of this soil
> Awake and fresh, so rich and royal
> It warms and thaws you—come now, wake
> Bring the Spring for goodness sake

Spring weather should arrive within the next week or two.

Mother Nature's Weather Predictions

The spring arrival wait is also a good time to learn how to predict the weather. It's a real plus for gardening enthusiasts. It helps to know when rain is on its way, when the first frost will arrive, and whether the coming winter will be exceptionally harsh. Personal weather knowledge helps us to plan ahead without worry of planting at the wrong time or missing that much-needed thunder shower. *Note:* To calculate the first frost, add six months to the date of the first thunderstorm of the year. The first Full Moon on or after that date will bring the first frost.

If you think you don't have time to bother with the art of prediction and would rather get the weather report from your local television station, so mote it be. But if your meteorologist is like mine, you probably can't remember the last time an accurate forecast was delivered. Sadly enough, if today's meteorologists would lift their eyes from the radar screen and shift them to Mother Nature, their weather reports would probably be a lot more precise. Why? Because Mother Nature tells us exactly what will happen from day to day. All we have to do is listen and watch for the signs.

As magical practitioners, we constantly strive toward complete harmony with Mother Nature. We already speak Her language and understand Her principles of balance. This makes weather prediction easier for us than for most other folks. All we have to know is what to look for.

The Moon is exceptionally helpful when it comes to predicting the weather, especially rain. For example, if the horns of the Moon point toward the Earth, rain will fall within three days. If a red Moon rises in the sky, it will rain the next day. When rain falls on the day of the Full Moon, showers are likely until She wanes to half. And, of course, if the Moon's reclining on Her back at the beginning of the fourth quarter, it will be a very wet week.

The most common weather signals and formulas are listed below for your convenience. Armed with this information, your weather forecasts will rival those of the most acclaimed meteorologists.

Signs of Approaching Rain

- A ring around the Moon

- Changes in the Moon's appearance on Sunday bring heavy rains

- Birds fly close to the ground

- The sun sets in clouds

- Ants cover the entrance to their anthill

- Smoke floats toward the ground

- Dandelion blossoms close

- Earthworms burrow out of the ground in large numbers

- Toadstools and mushrooms spring up overnight

- The leaves of cottonwood trees and clover rise upward toward the sky

- Flies appear inside the house and car

Signs of Fair Weather

- Smoke rises

- Crickets chirp more loudly than normal

- Locusts rub their wings together before nine o'clock in the morning

- A New Moon in winter rises in the south

- Morning clouds during the Waning Moon bring afternoon sunshine

- Screech owls screech

Signs of a Hard Winter

- Tough onion and apple skins

- Dogwood blooms excessively

- Berry vines bear an exorbitant amount of fruit

- An overabundance of pine cones or other evergreen fruit

- Leaves fall from the trees late in autumn, or fall before they change color

- Pine cones open early

- Apple trees bear fruit early

- Animals grow their winter coats early

- Tree bark is heavier on the north side

- Summer anthills are large and tall

- Squirrels build their nests closer to the ground and gather nuts in September

- Beaver dams have more logs on the north side than the south

Signs of a Mild Winter

- Thin skins on apples and onions

- Dogwood and berry blossoms are thin and sparse

Signs of a Hot Summer

- Birds mate and build nests before March 1

- Birds lay eggs three or four times during the spring instead of just twice

- Animals shed their winter coats early in the spring

Signs of an Abundant Harvest

- The first snow sticks to the trees

- Abundant snowfall throughout the winter months

- A white Christmas

Windsock Workings

If you've become a real pro at weather prediction and spring still hasn't sprung, take a good hard look at your windsock. It's much more than an attractive decoration. Used properly, it can become one of the most valuable magical tools in your assortment. All you have to do is learn how to use it.

Although we don't often think about it, the winds are strong and powerful, and can be harnessed to intensify magical workings. They are especially helpful when it comes to gardening magic.

The Winds

Air comes in many forms, but the most powerful type is wind. This is because it can change its intensity with the bat of an eye. There are gentle winds, breezy winds, and raucous, blustery, stormy winds. Winds can playfully twirl your skirt one minute and knock you off your feet the next. Winds are unpredictable. Everchanging. They form an energy with a power so raw that it's unsurpassed by any other natural force. Even better, they can easily intensify your magic. All you have to do is learn how to harness and apply them.

The trick to using the winds in magic is understanding that their magical vibrations differ according to the directions from which they blow. In short, the strength of the wind doesn't matter; it only matters whether it's coming from the east, south, west, or north. Want to harness the winds but don't know which way they're blowing? No problem. Just hang a windsock in your garden or outside a frequently observed window.

East Wind

This wind provides the proper energy for efforts that relate to metamorphosis, transformation, and change. It also boosts workings that involve beginnings, fresh perspectives, inspiration, communication, and creation. Use it to start new ventures, make plans, and form new relationships, as well as for aid in personal growth issues.

South Wind

Although southerly winds are most commonly harnessed for emotional issues like love, passion, and lust, don't sell them short. They also provide the perfect energy for workings that involve tenacity and determination, courage of conviction, physical vitality, and initiative. Try them, too, for resolving personal problems like selfishness, poor attitude, anger, and jealousy.

West Wind

Because of the healing, purifying quality of westerly winds, they provide the proper energy for resolving both physical and emotional issues. Use them to clear the mind and strengthen the intuition to bring about mental and physical efficiency, fertility, and productivity.

North Wind

Northerly winds are cold and strong, and bring about the perfect conditions for handling issues of a practical nature. Use this energy for dealing with matters that involve clarity of mind, legal issues, home management, and financial matters. Try it, too, as a planning period for magical efforts you intend to work when the wind changes.

While working with the winds can really boost magical work, there may come a time when you need a particular wind direction and it just won't cooperate. What then? Just take a few minutes to visualize the wind blowing from the necessary direction, then say the chant below with feeling:

Spirit of the (East/South/West/North) Wind, arise
Grab some gusto from the skies
Do your thing and do it fast
Bring me what I need at last

Thinning and Strengthening

By the time you get to this section, your seedlings should be thriving. In fact, if they have two sets of leaves, they're probably crowding each other. This means they're ready to thin. I have to admit that I've always had trouble with this part of the gardening process. I was taught early on not to waste, and that every-thing has a purpose. Simply put, throwing away perfectly good plants makes me feel as if my mother—hands on her hips and lips pursed in disapproval—is watching me from two thousand miles away. Still, it has to be done. Otherwise, it's likely that none of the plants will survive.

The basis for thinning new plants is a good one. If seedlings are too crowded, the roots fight for food and water. The soil becomes compacted. Air can't circu-late. And before you can say "Goddess bless!" your once healthy little sprouts topple flatly to their demise. The main idea is to have only one plant per pot. That way, each sprout gets plenty to eat and enough room to grow.

Thinning your plants isn't difficult, and it doesn't have to make you feel guilty. It can be a little messy, though, so you might want to grab some newspaper to use as a work surface. Grab some extra pots, cell-packs, and sterile potting mix while you're at it. That way, you don't have to throw any sprouts away. Just pot them and share them with your friends. The tips below will get you started.

- If seedlings are growing in plastic pots or cell-packs, squeeze the sides of the container toward the center to loosen the soil. Place your hand over the top of the pot, turn it upside down, and give the bottom a firm tap. The plants and soil should come out in a fairly solid piece.

- If you planted seeds in clay pots, you'll need a dinner knife. Carefully slide the blade down the inside edge of the container until you reach its bottom, and gently move the knife in a clockwise motion until you reach the starting point. Then place your hand over the top of the pot, turn it upside down, and tap it firmly.

- Gently crumble the soil between your fingers and separate the plants. (Be careful during the separation process. New root systems are fragile and easily damaged.)

- Plant each sprout in its own pot while saying something like:

I give you room to grow
I give you air to breathe
I give you space to eat and sleep
I bless your life with ease

That's all there is to it. In no time at all, your plants will be well on their way to a strong, healthy existence, and they'll have you to thank. So will your friends and neighbors.

The Cold Frame

When sprouts have six to eight pairs of leaves, they're ready to be introduced to their permanent residences. Most gardeners call the outdoor introductory process *hardening off.* Hardening off is important because tender seedlings are just that. Tender. No matter how lush they grow or vibrant they seem, they don't yet have the strength or stamina to brave heavy winds or pouring rain, much less severe cold or heat. They need a little time to toughen their stems and leaves, and become acclimated to the freedoms of their new lifestyle. This process usually takes about a week.

There are probably as many techniques to acclimate seedlings as there are gardeners, but I think the most practical one involves the cold frame. The cold frame is a box—sometimes bottomless—with a clear lid that can be raised and lowered. While you can purchase a frame at most nurseries or build one your-self, a simpler, more inexpensive solution is available. All you need is a heavy plastic sweater box with a clear snap-on lid, and some small rocks or gravel.

Take the box outdoors and pour in approximately one inch of gravel. Set the plants on top of the gravel and chant something like:

Tender plants that flex and bend
Toughen up your leaves and stems
Learn to live this life anew
Grab hold, gain strength, and power, too

Let the box sit outside. (Unless you're experiencing extreme weather—gale force winds, heavy rains, excessive heat, or frosty nights—there's usually no need to cover the box.)

Another acclimation method is just as simple, but requires a little more effort on your part. Take seedlings outside for one hour the first day, then increase the outdoor time each day by thirty minutes. Since seedlings are baby plants and are more delicate than those you might purchase in a nursery, remember to keep them away from frost, bright sunshine, and windy areas.

It doesn't matter which method you choose. Both work equally well. The only important thing to remember is to water the plants as you normally would. In seven days, they should be sturdy enough to hold their own in the garden.

Getting Started Indoors.
Working with Moon Phases and Moon Signs

Just as for outdoor herbs, the appearance of six to eight sets of leaves on indoor plants signals that the time has come to introduce them to their permanent homes. In all honesty, this process is much easier than that for outside plants. There's no hardening off to tackle, no cold frame involved, and no worry about excessive heat or cold. Because the herbs are already used to their environment, all you have to do is transplant them and let Mother Nature taker Her course. Something you may want to consider though—before you prepare a permanent residence for your plants—is the phase of the Moon and Her current astrological ascendant.

Planting (or transplanting) in the proper phase of the Moon is crucial to successful gardening. This is because not all plants are alike. They need different energies and environments to thrive, and the Moon is capable of providing exactly what each type needs. Use the list of phases below as a guideline, and your garden will always grow lush and green.

Dark to Waxing

Use this phase to plant herbs that grow above the ground and reseed themselves. A few examples are dill, sunflowers, chamomile, poppies, lavender, and thyme.

Waxing to Full Moon

This phase works wonders for plants that grow above the ground and form seedpods and berries. A few examples of these are beans (vanilla, tonka, castor, and so on), sweet peas, juniper, rowan, and pine.

Full to Waning Moon

Any plant that grows below the ground—bulbs and root crops fall into this category—will benefit when planted during this phase. A few examples are irises, daffodils, carrots, radishes, ginseng, and ginger.

Waning to New Moon

Avoid planting at this time; instead, use this phase for weeding.

The Moon's astrological sign is just as important to the planting process as the Moon phase. It can mean the difference between strong, healthy herbs or a wilting, withering mess. While there are countless ways to calculate the sign of the Moon, I find most of them so complicated that I'd never get my plants in the ground if I had to do my own figuring. For this reason, I cheat, and unless you have a strong base in astrology, I strongly suggest that you do, too. All you need is a good ephemeris or almanac. The information is already processed and calculated for you. Just look it up next to the date in question.

When the Moon phase is in harmony with what you want to plant, check it against the Moon's current astrological sign. Then use the list below to determine whether or not it's a good time to plant. *Note:* Plants can be successfully set out or potted up during any fruitful or neutral sign.

FRUITFUL SIGNS: Although every plant enjoys the energies of these signs, they are especially beneficial to those that produce flowers, pods, and berries.

Cancer, Scorpio, Taurus, Sagittarius, Pisces

NEUTRAL SIGNS: These signs carry a more subtle vibration, but still are of benefit to all plants. I like to use their energies when working with leafy herbs.

Libra, Capricorn, Aquarius

BARREN SIGNS: Try to avoid planting or transplanting during these signs. Their energies are best used for weeding, trimming, and cutting back.

Aries, Gemini, Leo, Virgo

The Strawberry Pot

Now that you know when and when not to transplant, you're ready to move your plants to their permanent homes. Before you do, though, you may wish to consider a couple of alternative indoor gardening ideas. One of them involves the use of a strawberry pot. Usually made of clay, these pots provide a great way to display your herbs. And because there are multiple openings on the sides of these containers, you can grow lots of plants in minimal space. Without a doubt, these pots are the indoor gardener's dream come true.

Strawberry pots work well with nearly any type of herb. (The only exceptions are mints and those herbs that have rhizomes instead of root systems. For these types, please see the section on Conventional Potting.) Some ideal candidates are marigolds, ivy, lavender, sage, parsley, basil, thyme, rosemary, sweet marjoram, oregano, and lady's mantle. If you'd like to work with strawberry pots, try the tips below. You'll not only be amazed at the beauty of your garden, but at the multitude of plants you can successfully grow.

Purchase a piece of one-inch plastic pipe (available in the plumbing section of the hardware store) for each pot to be used. Cut the pipes the same length as the depth of the pots.

- Using an ice pick, carefully poke several rows of holes down the length of the pipe. Insert the perforated pipe in the center of the pot, and add an inch or so of gravel or small pebbles.

- Fill the container with potting mix, stopping to transplant your seedlings as you reach the side holes. Carefully tamp down the soil around each plant, saying something like:

> *I plant you here now, little sprout*
> *Grow green and strong—let your roots stretch out*
> *Enjoy your home; thrive easily*
> *As I will, so mote it be*

- Give your plants a thorough watering by pouring water down the pipe. Repeat whenever the soil on top is dry to the touch.

- Fertilize once a month with compost tea (see recipe) or liquid fertilizer. Just pour the solution down the pipe as you would for normal watering.

Gardening with Hydroponics

Another idea for indoor gardeners is to create a water garden with the use of hydroponics. Don't let the word scare you. Hydroponics is just a fancy term for growing plants in water instead of soil. And believe it or not, herbs thrive in this type of environment. The reason for this is simple: In the conventional garden, all plant nutrients must be converted to liquid for root absorption. With hydroponics, no conversion is necessary. Other benefits include the absence of soil-borne diseases, mildew, weeds, and insect-related problems. In fact, the only drawback to hydroponics is that you cannot use the system to germinate seeds. In order for it to work successfully, you must garden with seedlings.

The Hydroponic System

While you can purchase a hydroponic system through mail order, it really isn't necessary. Creating your own is easy, inexpensive, and gratifying. Just follow the directions below.

2 plastic tubs or large plastic mixing bowls (one should be
    slightly larger than the other; the idea is for there to be
    at least a 2-inch bottom clearance in the larger container
    when the smaller one nests inside of it)

6 strips of polyester fabric cut 1-inch wide and 6-inches long
    for wicks

Ice pick

Sharp craft knife

Liquid fertilizer

Vermiculite, sphagnum moss, pebbles, or gravel

Seedlings

Start by turning the smaller container upside down on a flat surface. Then use the ice pick to poke 6 evenly spaced holes in the bottom.

Use the craft knife to enlarge the holes to approximately one-half inch.

Thread a fabric strip through a hole so that half the length rests inside the container and the other half, outside. Repeat with the other wicks.

Turn the container right side up and fill it half full with vermiculite, sphagnum moss, pebbles, or gravel.

Completely remove all soil from seedling root systems. (An easy way to do this is to soak the soil away in a sink of tepid water.)

Place the plants in the container, then finish filling it with the sphagnum moss, vermiculite, pebbles, or gravel. As you plant, use the chant described in the Strawberry Pot section.

Following the directions on the package, prepare two quarts of liquid fertilizer. If you'd rather use compost tea, just dillute one quart of tea with one quart of water. (See compost tea recipe on the next page.)

Place the smaller container inside the large one, and pour the fertilizer evenly over the plants. (At this point, you may want to lift the planted container slightly to see if the wicks are resting in the fertilizer solution. If not, mix up a little more fertilizer and add it to the upper container until the wicks are at least partially covered by the liquid.)

Give yourself a pat on the back! You've just created your very own water garden.

Maintaining the hydroponic garden is just as simple as creating it. All you have to do is mist the plants every day and keep a close eye on the liquid levels in the bottom container. When the levels reach one inch, just pour some more fertilizer over the upper container. A few words of caution, though: Plants grow much more quickly in a hydroponic environment, so they'll need trimming more often than their soil-bound counterparts.

Conventional Potting

If neither of the ideas listed above have much appeal, then conventional indoor gardening is for you. There's nothing wrong with that. As much as I like the more unconventional methods, there's something both comforting and invigorating about an assortment of lush, thriving herbs living happily on the windowsill and countless other areas of the home. If this appeals to you, too, grab some gravel or pebbles, some potting mix, and your sterile pots. With the directions below, your seedlings will have new homes in no time flat.

- Herbs thrive in well-drained soil. To assure good drainage, add approximately one inch of pebbles or gravel to the bottom of each pot.

- Fill each pot half full with potting mix.

- Remove seedlings from their current containers using the method described in the Thinning and Strengthening section. *Note:* To avoid confusion, it's a good idea to work with one seedling at time during the transplanting process.

- Nestle the seedling in the pot and finish filling with potting mix to secure it. As you plant the seedling, use the chant described in the Strawberry Pot section.

- Label the plant, place the pot on a plastic saucer, and water thoroughly.

- Whenever the top soil feels dry to the touch, water by filling the saucer. Using the same method, fertilize once each month with compost tea or liquid houseplant fertilizer.

Compost Tea

Compost tea is just what it sounds like; it's a liquid form of compost or farm manure. Used full strength, it does wonders for the roots of outdoor plants. Diluted to the color of weak tea, it makes a fabulous fertilizer for indoor plants and a nutritious mist for outdoor blossoms and leaves.

To prepare the tea, place one to two level shovels of farm manure or compost in a burlap bag. (Mesh laundry bags work well for this, too.) Tie the top of the bag and toss it into a large bucket of water. Chant something like:

Revive as I recycle you
Left over waste, gain life anew

Let the tea steep for seven days, using the chant at least once each day. At the end of the week, remove the bag and charge the tea by saying something like:

I charge you, tea, with might and power
To feed my roots, leaves, and flowers
Do your thing and make plants grow
As I say, it will be so

Magical Help for Indoor Plants

Now that you've found the perfect environment for your indoor plants and have placed them in permanent homes, it's time to let you in on a little secret: Indoor gardening provides you with an opportunity that outdoor gardening does not. An opportunity to boost the magical energy properties of your plants beyond belief. It's quick and easy, but best of all, it's inexpensive. All you have to do is take advantage of it.

First, list your plants on a piece of paper, then write their magical properties and associations beside them. (If you're not sure which properties go with which plants, check appendix D in the back of the book.) Next to that, jot down the stones appropriate to the properties. (Check appendix G for this information.) Lavender, for example, might look something like:

Plant	Magical Properties	Appropriate Stones
Lavender	Anger Management	Amethyst
		Carnelian
	Love	Amethyst
		Rose Quartz
	Protection	Citrine
		Lepidolite

Once you've made the list, decide whether you want to strengthen all of the herb's magical properties or just one. (If you're not sure exactly how you'll be using the plant in magic, I suggest boosting them all. After all, an herb enchanted specifically for anger management might not do you much good as a general protective device!) Then choose a few stones to suit your purpose. Taking lavender as an example, the most inexpensive way to charge the herb would be to use amethyst for both anger management and love, and add citrine for protection. Of course, it's perfectly all right to use as many stones as you like.

Next, find a store that carries stone beads or drilled stone chips. Stores that specialize in hobbies or arts and crafts are usually good bets. (Failing that, you can purchase stone beads by mail order.) While you're at the store, pick up some beading needles and monofilament thread.

Now for the fun stuff! Cut a length of thread a foot or two long, thread the needle, and tie a knot in the end. Then string on the stones, enchanting them as you work. While stringing amethyst for anger management, you might chant something like:

> *Dissolve all anger, stress-free stone*
> *This power to my lavender, loan*

For love, try:

> *Stone of love and perfect rapture*
> *This property allow my lavender to capture*

And for protection:

> *Stone of protection that endures*
> *This property within my lavender secure*

Thread as many stones as you like, chanting as you go. Tie a slip knot in the end of the thread, and hang it above the lavender. As the herb grows toward the charged stones, its magical properties will grow as well.

The Balancing Act

While you're waiting for the seedlings to harden off, take some time to go over your garden plans again. Look at the planting arrangements, then pay some special attention to your plant lists to see if they're balanced. Balanced? Yes! Like every other form of magic, planting the magical herb garden should involve the focused balance of Element and male and female rulerships.

Balancing the herb garden is simple. It doesn't mean that you have to take plants off your list. It only means that you may need to add a few to set things straight. Depending on the type of garden you have in mind—love, protection, or prosperity, for example—you may only have to equalize the male and female energies. For magical gardens with more than one purpose, though, it's a good idea to give each Element a fair shake as well. That way, you reap the total benefit of Nature's cosmic energy.

To start with the balancing act, check your plant list against the appropriate appendixes in the back of this book. Jot down the rulership beside each plant listed, then check to see if you have an equal number of each. If not, go through the rulership list again and search for familiar plants to add to your assortment.

But what if you don't want to plant anything else? What if you don't have the space? Or you like your planting arrangements just as they are and don't want to change them? Don't despair! There's another way to put things into balance without messing up your plans. Adding some symbols to your garden can easily fix the problem, too.

For example, a Goddess deficiency can be remedied by placing a pot of a feminine-ruled herb in the center of the garden. Other ideas might include a small goddess figure, an assortment of seashells, or holy stones. A bird bath or fountain—though this is admittedly more expensive—would rectify the problem, as well.

If you have a flagstone walkway in the garden, you've already managed to hold any God deficiency problems at bay. If not, try a centrally located god figure, some crystals, a phallic symbol (a plaster mushroom might work well for this), or a tall standing stone.

Element deficiencies are just as easily resolved. Some ideas are listed below to help you get started. (While some items on the lists are designed to beautify the garden area, others are simply symbols suggested to achieve balance. Feel free to bury any symbols you don't want to look at everyday.)

AIR: Windsock, plastic or paper fan, pinwheel, ribbon streamers, bird statue, a piece of orange calcite or citrine.

WATER: Seashells, mermaid statue, small fountain, soaker hose, a piece of aquamarine or lapis lazuli.

FIRE: Sun dial, statue of a Sun god or goddess (or a likeness of the Sun), a couple of burned wooden matches, a piece of carnelian or sunstone.

EARTH: Crystals or moss agate, a likeness of the Green Man, copper pennies, acorn caps, pine bark mulch, a light sprinkling of top soil.

Once you've decided which equalizers to use, enchant each one separately by saying something like:

> *Symbol of (Air/Fire/Water/Earth), I give you new clout*
> *I charge you now to equal things out*
> *Be true to your Element—be true to your form*
> *Bring things into balance and back to the norm*

Bury or place the item in the garden area.

By now, spring has probably sprung and, if you're like me, your thumbs are turning greener by the minute. You have the urge to transplant your seedlings. The garden is calling you, luring you, and you think you can't wait one more minute. If this sounds anything like you, take a deep breath and relax. There's one more thing you have to do before you set out the seedlings. It won't take long, but it's a necessity. You have to check the garden soil and make sure it's as ready as you are.

Simply put, the ground should be soft and crumbly. Test it by using your hands. If you can scoop out areas to set plants, it's ready. If not, grab the hoe or tiller, turn the soil again, and give it a good raking. It won't take long, and it's well worth the effort.

Dealing with Pesky Critters

If spring has truly arrived, a second hoeing may not be your biggest worry. You may find evidence of birds, deer, rabbits, moles, gophers, and field mice. Those delightful little critters that simply revel in stripping your plants of foliage and devouring them from the roots up. If that's the case, don't despair. Just perform the rituals outlined on the following pages. They're guaranteed to chase away even the most stubborn garden pests.

Mole, Gopher, and Field Mouse Begone Ritual

Several empty glass bottles (beer and soda pop
bottles work well for this)
Small amount of cornmeal

Take the bottles and cornmeal out to the garden, then stand in the center of the area and ask the Quarter Guardians to bless you with Their presence. Invoke Them by saying something like:

East and West and North and South
Hear what issues from my mouth
Come at once into this place
And bless me with Your loving grace

Once you feel Their presence (this may take a few minutes), explain that you have no beef with the little critters; they just need to find another place to live. Then chant something like:

Guardians All, now hear my plea
Take these critters far from me
They're small and cute and have their place
In the scheme of life and Nature's race—
But help them find another home
Where without danger, they can roam

Go to a mole or gopher tunnel or a mouse nest near the garden edge. Turn a bottle upside down and push it into the ground, neck first. Continue pushing until the bottom of the bottle is flush with the ground surface. As you push, say:

Bottle, echo in the ground
Magnify each single sound
Until these critters run away
And find another place to stay

Plant bottles at six to ten foot intervals along the tunnels, saying the chant as you go.

When all the bottles are in place, talk to the offending ground dwellers. Say something like:

Live your life freely—live your life well
Outside the realm of this plot you must dwell
Find a new home immediately
Merry now part, and blessed, please be

Leave the center of the garden and walk to the Northern Quarter. Sprinkle a bit of cornmeal there, thank the Guardians for their assistance, and ask for Their continued support. Say something like:

Thank you, North Guardians, for lending an ear
And for your help with the problem here
Please guard this spot from pests below
As I will, it shall be so

Traveling widdershins (counterclockwise), repeat the process with each Quarter.

Rabbit and Deer Away Ritual

2 pair old pantyhose
   Hair clippings (procure these from your local hairstylist)
   Scissors

Cut the panty and feet portions from the pantyhose and discard, then cut the remaining four tubes in half. Tie a knot in one end of each tube to form a bag, then stuff each bag full of hair. As you stuff, say something like:

Human hair, I conjure you
Breathe again—gain life anew
Secure protector you shall be
By Star, Moon, Sun, and Shining Sea

Secure the open ends with a knot, then take the bags to your garden plot. Place the first bag at the Northern Quarter and say something like:

Do now what I ask of you
Guard this place from pests that chew
(Like cute rabbits and pesky deer)
Keep them far away from here

Traveling widdershins, repeat the process at the Western, Southern, and Eastern Quarters. Still working widdershins and starting with the Northeast Quadrant, lay the remaining pouches between the Quarters. As you place each pouch, say something like:

With magic, now, this Quarter's crossed
So no protection shall be lost
These boundaries be securely held
By human scent and magic spell

When the last pouch is in place, return to the Northeast Quadrant. Traveling widdershins, completely circle the garden boundaries once more while saying:

From Circle boundary 'round about
Four-legged friends must all stay out
Outside this line, I wish you well
With joy and love, I set this spell

Bird Flyaway Ritual

All you need for this ritual is an assortment of toy pinwheels. If your garden is planted in rows, get two for each row. Otherwise, the number is up to you. All that's important is that you have enough to space them at three to four foot intervals around your garden area. As you push each pinwheel in the ground, chant something like:

Spin this wheel, O gentle breeze
Confuse all birds now, so they flee
Spin it fast and hard and long
So I'm graced with nothing but their song

When you have placed the last pinwheel in the ground, stand in the center of the area and say:

My feathered friends, I love you each
But these plants must stay out of your reach
Go now and find a happy home
And leave this garden plot alone

Purchased Plants: How to Find Healthy Ones

Some plants just don't grow well from seed. If you run into this problem—or you need some plants to fill in garden areas—a few starter plants from the local nursery may be in order. Sometimes, though, it's hard to tell which plants are healthy and which plants aren't. This is because nearly everything seems to thrive at the nursery. If you can't decide which plants to take home, follow the three simple steps below. They're guaranteed to help you make good choices toward a lush, healthy garden.

- Take a good look at the plant leaves and stems. Check the leaf undersides, too. Only consider those plants that have sturdy stems and are free from yellow, brown, or white spots and yellowing leaves.

- Inspect each plant again—this time for insects. If you see anything that crawls or flies, put the plant down immediately. The last thing you want is to infest your entire garden.

- Gently squeeze the sides of the pot and carefully lift the plant out. Check the root system for size, color, and flexibility. If the root system is small, brown, and stiff, it's not for you. Choose plants that have a well-formed, white root ball.

That's it! All that's left is the fun stuff. Just take your new plants home, trim any roots peeking out from the bottom of the pot, and give them a permanent living space.

Transplanting Seedlings Outdoors

With the soil ready and your plant-devouring friends on the move, you can transplant seedlings and purchased plants to your heart's content. Your seedlings are probably still a little delicate, so make plans to introduce them to the garden on a cloudy day or late in the afternoon. The sunlight isn't as harsh then, so you won't have to worry about it overheating plants or scorching their leaves. Other planting tips are listed below for your convenience.

- Carefully remove seedlings from their containers, then scoop out enough soil from your garden to set the plant and attached potting mix just beneath the surface line.

- Replace the soil around the plant loosely. Don't tamp it down. This allows for air circulation—a necessary provision for tender outdoor root systems. While replacing the soil, use the chant described in the Strawberry Pot section.

- When transplanting pennyroyal, mints, or other plants with rhizomes, pot them first in clay containers using the conventional potting method described previously. (It's a good idea to use a pot twice as large as you think they need. I usually use 6- to 8-inch pots for this.) Then scoop out the ground and transplant the plant in its container. This allows for plant growth without worry that the little rascals will conquer the entire garden. It also keeps the flavors and scents of these plants to themselves. There's nothing worse than discovering that your lemon balm smells and tastes like peppermint! For extra protection against this sort of thing, try the chant below as you set the plant in the garden:

> *Wild child, wild child, run and play*
> *But in this housing, you must stay*
> *Grow strong, grow proud, grow happily*
> *As I will, so mote it be*

- Mark each plant for future reference. You may know which plant is which right now, but herbs have a way of changing form as they mature. Use a waterproof marker and sturdy plastic strips for this.

- Use a watering can to give each plant a thorough soaking. Its saturation factor is much more effective than that of the hose, and it's important that the initial transplantation watering reach the roots. As you water, say something like:

Nutrients, now liquify
Reach the roots that lie nearby
So they will get just what they need
As from the Earth, they drink and feed

- Don't forget to save one area of the garden for the fairies to tend. Plant sturdy plants there—ones that aren't likely to be choked out by invading weeds. (Lavender, pinks, thyme, basil, violets, and lemon balm are good choices.) After the initial planting, don't weed it. Water and fertilize as you do the rest of the garden, but otherwise leave it alone. This gives the fairies an opportunity to grow what you need. Don't be surprised, though, if the plants that sprout there aren't normally indigenous to your area. Fairies—the garden's most magical creatures—have a way of manifesting that which is necessary, even when that manifestation is humanly impossible.

Garden Blessing Ritual

No one can expect their garden to thrive well without the essentials—and for magical practitioners, that includes the blessing of the Ancients. How you bless your garden is up to you. The ritual can be as informal or extensive as you like. It's important that that the blessing reflect your lifestyle, though. This assures the Ancients—and the garden plants—that you intend to keep your personal commitments to them, and handle every responsibility that might entail. For your convenience, a sample ritual is outlined on the following page.

Equipment

4 garden stakes
1 yard yellow ribbon
1 yard red ribbon
1 yard blue ribbon
1 yard green ribbon
 Optional symbols of Air, Fire, Water, and Earth,
  respectively (feather and/or a piece of citrine or
  orange calcite, charcoal briquette and/or a piece
  of sunstone or carnelian, seashell and/or a piece
  of aquamarine or lapis, small fern/plant and/or
  a piece of moss agate or aventurine)

Plant a stake at the east and tie the yellow ribbon to it. (If you opted for additional Air symbols, tie the feather to the ribbon or place the stone at the base of the stake, as well.) Sprinkle a little cornmeal around the stake and ask the Guardians to bless your garden by saying something like:

> *Guardians of Air, please come out to play*
> *Chase garden pests far, far away*
> *All negativity from this plot dispel*
> *Bring fertility into my garden as well*
> *I ask now Your blessings on this plot of ground*
> *Watch over it well; keep it thriving and sound*

Plant a stake in the south and attach the red ribbon. Place any additional Element symbols at the base of the stake, and add a bit of cornmeal as before. Then invoke the Guardians of Fire using the chant above.

Repeat the process at the west and north, then travel back to the east to close the circle. Walk to the center of the garden and chant:

> *Guardians of Air, Fire, Water, and Earth*
> *I invite you to live here in love and in mirth*
> *By magic of spell and the power in me*
> *Pour forth Your blessings! As I will, shall it be*

Alternative Garden Blessing Ritual

Garden seeds or plants
1 quart milk
½ cup honey
1 small tree or bush branch with newly sprouted
    leaves and buds
1 2-quart container
2 stakes or sticks for each garden row
Pastel ribbons (one for each stake)

Gather the materials and find a comfortable spot in the garden. Combine the milk and honey in the container, place the branch in the mixture, and set aside.

Place a stake in the ground at the beginning and end of each row, then transplant the plants. Tie a ribbon bow around each stake, saying to the plants in that row:

My gift to you is perfect love
Grow strong and tall toward the sky above

Using the branch, asperge the garden with milk and honey. Consecrate it by saying something like:

Milk and honey, flow throughout
Bringing richness to each seed and sprout
Lord and Lady, dance and play
Love and laugh here every day
So that everywhere you walk and skip
You bring lush growth from seed and pip

Water the garden thoroughly, and tend to its needs daily.

Growing, Hoeing, & Keeping Things Going

MOST FOLKS THINK THE MOST important part of gardening is the planting, but it just isn't so. The fact is, anyone can plant a garden. It takes real talent, however, to grow and maintain one. Don't think you have what it takes? Not to worry. That's where your personal magic and the help of the Ancients come in. Still concerned? Try the tips in this chapter. They're guaranteed to work—even for the most anxious of gardeners!

Before you can really begin to maintain your garden, it has to grow. While many things figure into the growth factor, the most important ones are adequate food, water, and stimulation. You can trust Mother Nature to take care of that if you like, but for real success, She has to consistently deliver the Elements in appropriate proportions. This seldom happens, so it's a good idea to lend Her a helping hand.

Give the Garden a Drink

The first step in obtaining luxurious growth is to make sure your garden gets enough water. This can be a tricky situation, since your garden plot—especially if it's clay-based like mine—may look dry on the surface but may actually be swimming in the wet stuff underneath. The truth of the matter is that every garden is different. What may be adequate for one could drown the

61

next. And that same amount of water could leave another garden dying of thirst. Sadly enough, there is no pat formula. What is adequate for your garden all depends on your climate, rainfall, and soil texture and content.

There is an easy way to take the guesswork out of watering, though, and all it takes is your thumb. Just poke it into the ground until the soil is about an inch of the way up. If the soil is dry, don't hesitate: Grab the hose and give your garden a nice long drink. Make watering the garden a magical act by chanting something like:

Water, rain from end of hose
Wash away all thirsty woes
Soak my plants—root, stem, and leaf
As I will, so mote it be

While watering with the hose is quite effective, there are times it just isn't feasible. Let's say, for example, that you live in a dry area and your garden needs daily moisture. Not a problem—unless, of course, you want to leave town for the weekend. While you may find a neighbor who's willing to come over and tend your thirsty plants, what if that person forgets? You'll come home to a parched garden full of scorched plants. Even worse, they may be too weak to revive. All your hard work just slid down the drain, and there's nothing you can do to fix it.

Fortunately, there's a quick and simple solution called drip watering. And all you need to implement this process is an ice pick and an assortment of one-gallon plastic containers. (Recycled milk jugs work well for this. If you're worried that you may not have enough containers, just ask your neighbors to save them for you. They'll be glad to. After all, it's much easier than trekking over to your house to water the garden!) With the ice pick, poke five or six holes in the container bottoms, line them up between the plant rows, and fill them to the brim with water. That's all there is to it. Not only will your plants get what they need, you'll be able to relax while you're gone.

Giving Herbs Some Breathing Room

When I was young, I used to watch the man next door play in his garden with a hoe. Of course, I thought it was a waste of time. The garden was already tilled. The plants were already growing. There wasn't a weed in sight. I remember thinking that he must just need an excuse for some quiet time. Since I wasn't exactly the quiet sort, I decided to leave him alone and not bother him.

If I'd had the good sense to open my mouth, my neighbor might have shown me a simple truth that took years for me to find. Fact is, gardens need regular hoeing whether they have weeds or not. It not only keeps the soil absorbent and accepting of moisture, but also provides necessary air circulation so your plants can breathe.

Plants need to breathe? You bet. When soil is packed, it forms a hard, solid, nearly impenetrable surface. Several days after a good rain, some soils become almost rocklike. The root systems pack, too, and there's no place for them to move. Instead of growing and branching out, they just sit there, still, immobile and stagnant. The air runs out and roots can't breathe. As a result, some plants just fall over and die.

When garden plots are turned and loosened on a weekly basis, though, plants get all the air they need. This makes for flexible, pliable soil that even tender root systems can push about. Since the environment is no longer restrictive, roots dig deep and branch out in all directions. They move and breathe freely, forming a base large enough to support their foliage. This definitely makes for healthier, happier plants.

Hoeing the garden doesn't have to be an unpleasant chore. You can always pass the time by singing the chants below to the tune of "Row, Row, Row Your Boat."

Hoe, hoe, hoe the Earth
Fill the soil with air
So the tender roots breathe well
And branch out everywhere
Turn, turn, turn the Earth
Magic's everywhere
As I will, so mote it be
In answer to my prayer

To Mulch or Not to Mulch

Since before I was old enough to garden, there's been much ado about mulch. Some gardeners swear by it. Others insist that it's not only a waste of time and money, but downright ridiculous. So, who's right? Who's wrong? Since both sets of gardeners seem to grow herbs successfully, an accurate determination isn't easy to make.

I, for one, like mulch. It covers the garden plot with an insulative blanket that's not only appealing to the eye, but protects tender roots from last minute spring cold snaps. It feeds the ground. It amends the soil. And for all practical purposes, plants just seem to be happier when covered in it. There's no reason to take my word for it, though. Read the list of mulching benefits below and decide for yourself.

- Mulch holds moisture in the soil. This means your garden needs less water. That's a plus, especially in hot, dry areas with little rainfall.

- Because mulch encourages the ground to absorb water, it easily keeps soil erosion problems at bay.

- Mulch helps, too, with weeding woes. Because weeds have to travel through it to obtain sunlight, all but a few die out before they reach the surface.

- Some mulches—compost, for one—feed beneficial soil organisms. Because it makes the soil richer and healthier, it can actually deter nasty fungal and viral disease from infecting your plants.

Best of all, mulching saves time. Without all that watering, weeding, and doctoring to do, you'll have plenty of time to sit back and enjoy your garden!

If you decide that mulching is for you, I recommend using compost. While other mulches are effective, many of them are chemically treated and can burn tender plants. Others don't decompose well and can form a breeding ground for harmful insects. Compost is completely organic, free (if you make it yourself), and simply chock-full of nutrients for your soil and plants. It's the best solution all the way around.

When mulching, spread the material across the garden plot evenly in a thickness of two to five inches. As you spread the mulch, chant something like:

Recycled stuff, now come alive
Help my garden to survive
Hold moisture in—hold weeds at bay
Erosion, too, chase clear away
And keep my plants free of disease
By Earth, Sun, Wind, and Shining Seas

Herbs Need Snacks and TLC

Some herb gardeners say that herbs don't need fertilizer. Experts tell me that they're naturally healthy plants, and sturdy enough to grab whatever they need from the soil. When my eyebrow shoots up in disbelief, they all remind me that herbs—no matter what their appearance or texture—are simply weeds. This, of course, is followed by the lecture to end all lectures, and the gist of it is that everyone knows better than to fertilize common weed plants.

While that may be somewhat true, I beg to differ. Fertilizing herbs is a little like feeding children. The average child survives beautifully on a steady diet of hot dogs and peanut butter sandwiches. But feed that same child a healthy diet on a regular basis, and see what happens. The child grows tall and strong, and with a speed so ferocious, it's guaranteed to make your head spin.

The same is true of herbs. Grown in their own natural habitat, they are tenacious little critters. They eat, they grow, and they survive. When you fertilize them, though, they tend to shoot up and bush out nearly overnight. Another reason to fertilize is that you'll probably plant at least a few herbs that aren't indigenous to your area. At the very least, this means that they'll need help adjusting to a foreign environment. But more likely than not, they'll also need nutrients that your local soil just doesn't have to give them. I can't think of a better reason to fertilize. Besides, all herbs—even those living in their natural environment—love fertilizer just as much as kids love candy.

While I've had exceptional results nurturing my herbs with fertilizer, finding the right one was often an effort in chaotic confusion. Many brands were too gentle for some plants and too harsh for others. Some just wouldn't do at all. For this reason, I started using compost tea (see the recipe in the Learning, Turning, and Discerning section), and two other organic fertilizers that are easily accessible and absolutely free.

One of the most overlooked and unrecycled organic propagators on this planet is something that virtually everyone has at home. It's more effective than any expensive growing aid on the market, yet we consistently flush it from our lives every day. Even better, it's simply saturated with nitrogen—the one growth ingredient that most plants lack. What is it? Surprisingly enough, it's human urine.

Preparing urine for garden use is just as easy as obtaining it. Just dilute it with tap water—a 1:1 ration works well—then pour it in your watering can to use on all your plants and seedlings. The results are usually apparent within three days.

Have tropical fish? Then you have another potent growing aid right at your fingertips. Recycled aquarium water is one of the best organic fertilizers in existence. Once a month, use a hose to siphon old aquarium water into the bathtub, then pour into your watering can and apply it liberally to your herb plants. Save any leftover water in a bucket and use it daily until it's gone.

It's a good idea to fertilize herbs once a month. You can just pour the solution on the ground around the plants, but I find that it's more effective to use a watering can. The reason behind this is that the force of the water pouring from the can is a gentle one. This allows you to feed the whole plant without worry of damage to tender stems and foliage. As the fertilizer pours forth, say something like:

> *Grow my children, grow strong and tall*
> *Roots reach out to grab nutrients, all*
> *Leaves eat, too, and stems grow strong*
> *Absorb all you need to thrive well and live long*

The Gardeners' Rede: Pull That Weed

I have to admit that up until a few years ago, I was no good at pulling weeds. I'd been brought up to believe that all life was good, all life was important, and all life had Spirit. To my way of thinking, pulling a weed was more than a travesty against Nature—it was murder, plain and simple.

The worst part of it was that my intelligence was above average. I knew that weeds gobbled up nutrients in the soil quicker than you could say, "Blessed be." Because of their voracious appetites, they grew healthy, tall, and strong. They branched out and multiplied. And when they ran out of room, they invaded other garden areas. Then they crowded the resident plants until they literally choked the life out of them. Sadly enough, I was too weak to do anything about it. I just chalked it up to the cycles of Nature, the survival of the fittest, and let it go at that. To my dismay, my garden was never the place of beauty or magical paradise I'd envisioned. It was nothing more than a glorified weed patch.

This doesn't have to happen to you. You just have to make up your mind not to be as passive as I was. Remember that as a gardener, you are the warrior of the plant world. So, stand tall. Stand firm. Stand proud. Know that it's your responsibility to protect the tender sprouts you planted, that it's up to you to defend them against invading weeds (no matter how pretty or harmless they may seem at the onset), that it's your job to see that your plants reach maturity and live a long and happy life. And the only way to do that is to stop weeds in their tracks by pulling them on sight.

Still feeling a little queasy about weed pulling? Try this chant. It's guaranteed to bring out the garden warrior in everyone.

> *Warrior Spirits, hear my cry*
> *As it soars to You on high*
> *Give me everything that I need*
> *So I can pull those nasty weeds*
> *And so with guilt I won't be ridden*
> *Bind Your strength to me unhidden*
> *Wrap it 'round me proud and well*
> *And seal its magic with this spell*

Then when it's time to go to battle—this is best done during Waning to New Moon—keep your courage up by chanting the following with each weed you pull.

> *I am Warrior—I am Strong*
> *I pluck out what does not belong*
> *I snatch you forth and stop you, weed*
> *By spell, begone and don't reseed.*

Waging the War on Flying, Crawling, and Creeping Critters

If your plants are healthy and get proper nourishment from the soil, you probably won't have a lot of trouble with bugs. This is because most herbs repel insects naturally. Once in a while, though, bugs can still get the best of you—and your garden. So, what's the solution? Should you pick bugs from plants as you find them? Unfortunately, that doesn't always work. In striving to fight insect infestation, many gardeners unwittingly rid their plants of beneficial bugs and critters. This leaves nothing to exterminate the eggs and larvae of the more harmful ones.

Because some herbs attract helpful insects and others repel those that are harmful, adding a few more garden plants might be a good solution. But what if you don't have room? Just pot a few from the lists below, then place them along the garden boundaries. This not only efficiently solves the pest problem, but adds beauty and versatility to almost any garden.

BENEFICIAL INSECT ATTRACTANTS: Chamomile, Dill, Fennel, Marjoram, Thyme.

HARMFUL INSECT REPELLENTS: Basil, Feverfew, Garlic, Lemon Balm, Lavender, Marigolds, Oregano, Pennyroyal, Sage, Tansy, Wormwood.

Heavy Artillery

Planting additional herbs is all well and fine, but what if your plants are already bug infested? No problem. You just need to pull out the heavy artillery. A weapon that's so slick, they'll never see it coming. What you need is a delectable eradicator made of herbs. The all-purpose organic pesticide recipes on the following pages will get you started. *Note:* Instructions for formula preparation follow after the recipes.

Fighting Fleabane Formula

  1 teaspoon dishwashing liquid
6½ cups water
  1 cup fresh fleabane roots and leaves, or 2 tablespoons
      dried fleabane roots and leaves

Wormwood Warlord Formula

1   teaspoon dishwashing liquid
6½ cups water
½   cup fresh wormwood leaves, or 1 tablespoon dried
     wormwood leaves

Note: It's best to use a glass pot when preparing these formulas. Metal is porous, and can soak up the natural oils that are essential for effective plant treatment.

Simmer the herbs in 4 cups of water for 30 minutes. As they simmer, chant something like:

> *Simmering herbs who art delectable*
> *Make your poisons undetectable*
> *Stop bugs dead—right in their tracks*
> *So my plants rest and relax*

Add 1 teaspoon of dishwashing liquid to 2½ cups of cold water with a teaspoon and mix well. Chant:

> *Soap and water, meld and gel*
> *Mix together very well*
> *Your adhesive qualities I call*
> *To stick to plant parts—leaves and all*

Add the soapy water to the decoction, let cool, and strain. Spray liberally on affected plants, while chanting something like:

> *Spray be stout, be warrior strong*
> *Work your magic hard and long*
> *Drop these bugs right where they lie*
> *Warrior spray, now hear my cry*

Aphids are stubborn critters and more difficult to eradicate than most garden pests. This is especially so if you have roses. For this reason, several aphid-specific formulas follow below. Unless otherwise specified, use the preparation instructions described on the previous pages for the all-purpose pesticides. The chants listed in that section apply to these formulae as well.

Screaming Banshee Formula

1 teaspoon dishwashing liquid
6½ cups water
1 cup fresh elder or rhubarb leaves, or 2 tablespoons
   dried elder or rhubarb leaves

Basil Bomber Formula

1 teaspoon dishwashing liquid
4 cups water
1 cup fresh basil leaves, or 2 tablespoons dried basil leaves

Add the basil leaves to 4 cups of boiling water. Let steep for 10 minutes. Strain the mixture when it cools, then add a teaspoon of dishwashing liquid. Spray on affected plants.

Garlic Guerrilla Formula

1 teaspoon dishwashing liquid
2½ cups water
2 cloves crushed garlic

Add the garlic to 2½ cups of boiling water. Let steep for 10 minutes. Strain the mixture when it cools, then add a teaspoon of dishwashing liquid. Spray on affected plants.

Waging the War on Slime

Of all the pests that sneak into my gardens, snails and slugs probably irritate me the most. It's not so much that I mind them having a bite to eat here and there, it's just that they are the most unmannerly constituents of the garden pest world. They creep out of hiding, slither along, and leave trails of slime wherever they go. And then, they don't even have the common decency to clean up after themselves. On a more serious note, snails and slugs can do an awful lot of damage to your plants. Mostly nocturnal creatures, they gobble away large portions of plant leaves in a single feeding—sometimes with such voracity that it may appear to be the work of rabbits or deer.

Fortunately, there are ways to get rid of them. You can sprinkle them with salt or crush them with your foot, but those solutions are definitely not for the squeamish. And either way, some of the slimers are bound to get away from you. Instead, try one of the trapping solutions below. They'll cure the problem and won't leave you feeling guilty.

Beer Trap

> A supply of wide-mouth jar lids
> Beer

Place a jar lid at every location you see plant damage. Flat side down, push the lid into the ground until it's flush with the surface. As you fill each lid with beer, chant something like:

> *Snails and slugs: come one, come all*
> *This beer's for you—now hear my call*
> *Have a drink; now suck it up*
> *And crawl into this tasty cup*

Check each lid the next day. Most of them will be filled with slimers. Dispose of the offending critters, then refill the lids. Repeat the process until the lids remain free of slimers for 24 hours.

Tube Trap

> An assortment of cardboard tubes
> Paper towels or newspaper

Lay the tubes in a horizontal position, and line the bottom halves with wet paper towels or newspaper. Place them in garden areas where damage is apparent. As you position each one, chant something like:

Snails and slugs, come right inside
Here's a place for you to hide
Make your home here; rest and be
Its dampness suits you perfectly

The next morning, check the tubes. Dispose of any with new tenants. Repeat the process until they remain empty for 24 hours.

The Horticultural Medic

Because garden maintenance is a multilevel project, there's more to it than being the ferocious garden warrior. It's a test of flexibility, creativity, and versatility. In short, you have to be able to change hats at a moment's notice. Usually, that means jumping into the role of horticultural medic.

All war invites casualties, and war in the garden is no exception. No matter how hard you fight or how well you defend, things are bound to happen. Some residents wind up with minor afflictions. Others are severely wounded. Either way, they need medical care. Care that only you can provide.

Now that I've got your attention, uncrease that brow and wipe the worried look from your face. A stethoscope isn't necessary. Neither is a degree in medicine. All you need is a watchful eye. Just check your plants on a regular basis and pay attention to any symptoms that might surface. The remedies that follow will take care of the rest.

Fungus Among Us

Fungal infections are the number one killer of young plants. While fungus can affect older plants, it most often attacks plants ranging from sprout size to one year of age. Heat, moisture, and cloudiness provide an excellent breeding ground for the disease, so it's very common in areas where those conditions prevail for extended periods of time. Symptoms vary, but the most common ones include leaves that turn yellow and die, and the sudden wilting of properly cared for plants. (Because lack of water can also cause these symptoms, you may want to thumb-check your soil before proceeding.)

As with all disease, the best way to take care of fungus is to prevent it. For your convenience, some preventative measures are listed below. If you suspect that your plants are already infected, try one of the organic fungicides that follow the prevention list.

- If your plants grow low to the ground and have leaves that touch the soil on a constant basis, remove the lower foliage.

- Prune any plants with weak stems. If they bend toward the ground instead of toward the sun, they could be good candidates for infection.

- Because fungus likes to hide in places where air doesn't circulate well, trim back any plants that are bushy in nature. Trimming will open the plant up a bit and will provide better aeration and drainage.

Chamomile Fungal Remedy

4 cups water
1 cup fresh chamomile flowers, or 2 tablespoons dried
    chamomile flowers

Add the chamomile to 4 cups of boiling water. Steep for 10 minutes and allow to cool. While the herbs steep, chant something like:

Herbs that chase disease away
Work your magic—let it stay
Within the bounds of this solution
Be powerful warriors of retribution

Strain the herb from the mixture, then spray liberally on affected plants. As you spray, chant something like:

Kill disease, O mighty spray
Bring my plants' health back today
Work your magic with speed and stealth
And protect my plants from more ill health

Horsetail Fungal Remedy

4 cups water
⅓ cup fresh horsetail, or 2½ teaspoons dried horsetail

Boil the horsetail in 4 cups of water for 20 minutes.

As the mixture boils, use the steeping chant for the Chamomile Fungal Remedy on the previous page. Cover and let stand for 24 hours before straining. Spray liberally on affected plants, using the spraying chant listed for the Chamomile Fungal Remedy.

Old-Fashioned Fungal Remedy

1 teaspoon baking soda
1 quart water

Dissolve the baking soda in the water. Pour the mixture into a spray bottle and liberally mist affected plants. (Use the chants listed in the Chamomile Fungal Remedy.)

If you've made it to this section, you deserve a break. By now, you're a multitalented, multifaceted gardener. You've learned to switch roles at the drop of a hat, and that's tough work—especially when the jobs involved are as challenging as those of parent, security guard, warrior, and doctor. Congratulations are in order, so give yourself a pat on the back. Then survey your garden and take a good look at all you've accomplished. Drink it in, suck it up, and be proud of yourself. It's one of the most gratifying moments you'll ever experience!

Garden Meditation

I like garden meditation because it serves many purposes. You can use it to relax and rejuvenate, to get rid of worries, and to dissolve old issues that get in the way. Its real powers lie elsewhere, though. The best reason to use the meditation has to do with attuning yourself to the herbs in your garden and discovering new ways to use them in magic.

It was while I was in this meditation that I discovered that sage—whose leaves I'd always used for purification—held some of the greatest psychic enhancement qualities of any herb in the plant world. For this reason, don't be surprised by anything you might learn. Above all, trust whatever knowledge comes to you. Plants never give advice without reason. All you have to do is use it.

Begin by taking a seat amongst your plants. Stroke their leaves, caress their stems, and let their fragrance fill the air. Then close your eyes, kick back, and relax. Take a deep breath and inhale the fresh, green energy of the plant world. Hold your breath for a count of ten, then exhale the metallic red energy of worries, stress, and aggravation. Let it sink into the Earth.

Continue to inhale green and exhale red until you're totally relaxed.

Eyes still closed, visualize your body changing. Your legs sprout roots and sink into the ground. They dig deeper and deeper into the safety of the moist, rich earth. Your torso changes, too. It becomes a sturdy, well-developed plant stem. Finally, your arms, shoulders, neck, and head change. Under the warmth of the Sun, they bud, sprout, leaf, and blossom.

Take a few moments to get used to your new form and life. Feel the breeze play through your leaves. Feel the sunshine warm your spirit. Let your roots travel through the earth in search of water and nutrition. Bask in your new surroundings. Enjoy being a plant.

Now that you're comfortable with your new living space, check out your neighbors. Start by introducing yourself to the plant closest to you. Ask who it is, and tell it about yourself. Find out what makes it happy. Find out what makes it sad. Get to know the plant a little better, then ask about its strong points and weak points. Ask about its magical vibrations, qualities, and purposes. Ask any other questions you might have, then close the conversation by telling the plant how glad you were to have met it, and that you hope your relationship will be a happy one. At this point you may continue one-on-one with other plants, or prepare to reenter the mundane world.

When you're ready to come back to the physical realm, stretch your arms, roll your neck, and shake off your leaves and blossoms. Twist your stem from side to side and feel it become a torso again. Let your roots travel up through the ground until they reach the surface and dissolve into your feet. Wriggle your toes. Flex the muscles in your legs. Give yourself a good shake. When your body feels normal again, stand up and leave the garden.

Note: Since it's a good idea to write down any information you've discovered during the meditation, you may want to keep a separate section in your notebook specifically for this purpose.

Harvesting the Bounty

The only thing more appealing than watching plants sprout and grow is the idea of finally reaping the harvest. From a practical point of view, it's a matter of seeing all your hard work come to fruition. But from a magical angle, it's more than that. Whether you want to admit it or not, there's something very exciting about harvesting real, live magic straight from the garden, then using it to reinvent your life.

One of the most magical things about herbs is that—unlike some other garden residents—you don't have to wait a full growing season to use them. The harvest season begins whenever you see fit and, with most plants, doesn't end until nearly a month before the first frost. This means you can consistently snip a sprig here and there without damaging plants and use it any time you want. In fact, harvesting herbs actually makes them grow better. That's definitely something to be excited about.

Since you'll want to get the most flavor, fragrance, and magical energy from the herbs you harvest, try the following tips. They'll go a long way in helping you achieve exactly what you desire.

- Pick a sunny morning to begin your harvest. This is important because plant leaves are more heavily laden with essential oils during morning hours.

- Wait until the dew dries. Harvesting wet or damp plants invites infection and disease.

- For magical potency at its best, harvest herbs just as they begin to blossom. Oils are more intensified during this period.

- To grab the most from herb flowers (chamomile, lavender, and so on) and their oils, harvest them just before they open.

- Use the right tool for harvesting. While some magical practitioners still prefer to use the boline, I find a pair of very sharp scissors much more useful. Why? Because scissors allow sharper, cleaner cuts, and a more precise cut not only aids the plant in healing, but encourages new growth.

- To strengthen the magical vibration of any herb, say an appropriate chant while harvesting. When harvesting an herb of protection like lavender, for instance, you might say something like:

> *Lavender, lend your strength and protection*
> *To secure magical efforts at my direction*

When plucking fluff heads from dandelions, though, the chant might be something more like:

> *Dandelion fluff, so wild and free*
> *Grant the wishes I ask of thee*

Harvest Thanksgiving Ritual

Perhaps the most important part of harvesting is remembering to thank your plants and the Earth. This ritual doesn't have to be anything fancy. It doesn't even have to be something formal. In fact, a sincere, spontaneous thank-you works as well as any fine-tuned ritual you could construct. The whole idea is to let them know you appreciate their efforts and their willingness to share themselves with you. If you're just not a spontaneous type of person, don't despair. Try the chant below. Not only will it do the trick—you and your benefactors will both feel better!

> *Giving plants and gracious Earth*
> *I give my heart in love and mirth*
> *For all You share so willingly*
> *I thank You, lush, green family*

While any sort of thank-you is perfectly acceptable, it's only good manners to reciprocate when someone's given you so much. For that reason, a little gift is in order. But how do you shop for Mother Earth and the plant world? Fortunately,

They're easy to please, so it's not that hard. I like to make a small offering of a strand of my hair or a fingernail clipping, which I plant in the Earth. Other ideas might include a few copper pennies, a bit of tobacco, or a smidgen of cornmeal.

Physical offerings aren't the only way you can go with this, though. If the ideas above don't appeal to you, try honoring your benefactors symbolically instead. Talk to Them and tell Them how wonderful They are, sing to Them, or blow Them a kiss. You might even light a green candle for Their continued health, or remember Them in your morning and evening prayers. What you give Them isn't the key factor here. All that's important is that your gift comes from the heart.

Preparing the Harvest

So the herbs are harvested and now you want to use them. It's only right. After all, you planned the garden. You planted it. You even learned to lovingly switch roles in midstream—often several times a day—to protect and nurture your plants. You did all the work, and it's your God or Goddess-given right to reap the benefits.

Not so fast! Before you grab those sprigs, a few preparations are necessary.

The first order of business is to wash your harvest. Whether you plan to use herbs fresh or dried, it's important to get rid of all the bugs, dirt, and microscopic crud. It won't take long, and it's well worth the effort. After all, there's nothing worse than having grit and grime in your food or medicine, or interlaced into your magical efforts.

- Begin by attaching a spray nozzle to your outside garden hose. Give herbs a good dousing, shake off any excess water, and bring them in the house.

- Place the harvest in a sink full of cold water. If herbs are limp, add a few ice cubes to revive them. Swish herbs around in the water for a few seconds, then let them soak for fifteen to twenty minutes. Chant something like:

> *Grit and grime and bugs, away*
> *Release your hold—you cannot stay*
> *Herbs, be cleansed; be fresh and new*
> *Keep flavors, perfumes, and powers, true*

- Remove the harvest from the sink and allow to drain in a colander. When most of the water has drained away, layer herbs between paper towels to soak up any leftover water.

Herb Drying Techniques

Once the herbs are clean, you're ready to move forward with the rest of the preparations. While some recipes specifically call for fresh herbs, they are few and far between. Dried herbs are more in demand. This is because drying seals the volatile, essential oils inside the leaves and stores it there for later use. Fact is, dried herbs are much more potent, fragrant, and flavorful than those used straight from the garden.

There are nearly as many ways to dry herbs as there are plant species. For your convenience, the most common methods are described below. All work equally well, so try the techniques that coordinate best with your lifestyle.

Microwave Method

Since the microwave oven dries herbs quickly, you'll want to use this method if you're in a hurry. The only drawback to nuking your herbs is that there's little time to enchant them further while they dry. This doesn't have to be a problem, though. Just chant while blotting away any excess water. If you were enchanting comfrey with additional healing powers, for example, you might say something like:

Herb that heals with most potent power
I command you—grow stronger by minute and hour
Until your powers reach full capacity
As I will, so mote it be

Afterward, place a layer of herbs between two sheets of paper toweling, then place a layer of herbs on top. Cover with another paper towel, and heat on high for forty-five seconds. Check the herbs. If the leaves are crisp, they're ready. If not, replace the paper towels and continue to heat at twenty second intervals until the leaves crumble easily.

Food Dehydrator Method

Because the food dehydrator is so versatile, its virtues don't stop at popping out jerky and fruit roll-ups. It's also incredibly effective for drying plant parts. Just spread a single layer of herbs on each tray and follow your manufacturer's instructions. That's all there is to it. Your herbs will be ready to use in a matter of hours.

Gas Oven Method

Want your kitchen to smell great while you're drying the harvest? Then try the gas oven method. Just place single layers of herbs on cookie sheets, pop them into the oven, and set the dial for 100 degrees. Then chant something like:

Dry, little herbs. Dry crisply, please
Seal all oils within your leaves
Hide them well until the time
I invoke them for magical reason and rhyme

Repeat the chant as you see fit. Check on the plants every couple of hours to see if they're ready, and remove those that are. This method takes a little longer than the two mentioned above, but herbs are usually ready for use in twenty-four hours or less.

Air Drying Method

Although this method doesn't work as quickly as the others I've mentioned, it's incredibly simple. In fact, there's very little that can go wrong. That's probably why folks use this technique more often than any other. Just use a rubber band to secure few plant stems together—no more than ten or twelve stems—and hang them in a cool, dark place to dry. (Using the chant described in the Gas Oven Method on a daily basis seems to hasten the drying process.) To prevent losing stray seeds from plants with pods, tie a paper sack around seeded areas. One note of caution, though: Don't forget to clearly label your bunches. There's nothing worse than adding catnip to a recipe that calls for catmint!

Once the herbs are dry, you'll need to strip the leaves and flowers from the stems (unless you plan to use full stalks for decorative or magical projects).

Because this job can be a little messy, you may want to spread a few sheets of newspaper over your work area. Set the stems aside and place the plant material in labeled jars with tight-fitting lids. If storage space is a problem, try plastic zippered bags. They not only keep herbal oils from evaporating, but take up much less room.

Don't throw away the stems when you're finished. They have lots of uses, so tie them into small bundles and store them, too. Later, you can toss them in the fireplace to make your house smell good, use them in stove-top potpourri, or burn them as a general cleansing incense. (To use them for wish magic, see the section on Herbs in the Magical Realm in part two.)

Storing Fresh Herbs

Drying herbs is all well and fine, but there are times when I really want to use fresh herbs for cooking. It's not a problem during harvest season. I can just run out and snip off whatever I need. The dilemma occurs much later. It's usually about the time there's a foot of snow on the ground and not much left of the garden but a memory. There's nothing to do but use dried herbs and wish fervently for fresh. Right?

Wrong! Over the years, I picked up a couple of tips for storing fresh herbs. They're quick. They're easy. But best of all, you'll have the luxury of fresh herbs for cooking any time you want. *Note:* Fresh herbs keep forever, but tend to lose their color and crispness after storage. Improper color doesn't mean they're no good!

- After washing, just chop herbs with a sharp knife. Place them in plastic zippered bags, squeeze out excess air, and seal tightly. Then label and toss in the freezer for later use.

- Grab some empty ice trays and place one teaspoon of chopped herb into each cube opening. Fill with water and freeze. Pop out the herb cubes, place them in plastic zippered bags, label, and return to the freezer. Add a cube or two to soup, stew, gravy, and sauce recipes. (For other herbal use ideas, see part two of this book.)

Plant Propagation Methods

The harvest season is more than just a period of magical and personal gratification. It also provides an excellent time to start thinking about next year's plans—especially if you want to keep the current garden residents and just add a few companions. While most plants weather the winter months just fine in my area, they may not in yours. This leaves you, the magical gardener, with several options. If you have an overabundance of time and space, you can dig up all your plants, put them in pots, and bring them inside until spring. If you don't want to bother with that, you can start over in the spring with new plants. If neither of these appeal to you, try the alternative I usually take: Just start new plants from the ones you already have. If you plant them in cell-packs or small pots, they won't take up much space.

Starting Cuttings

Plants can be propagated in a number of ways. My great aunt used to place root cuttings in jars of water. Her success rate was phenomenal. I tried this once or twice, but never had much luck. My cuttings turned brown, the stems grew spindly, and mush formed on the bottoms instead of roots. When I whined to Aunt Myrtle about the problem, she just laughed and said I had black thumbs. I finally gave up on the whole idea.

What Aunt Myrtle didn't tell me nearly cost me the pleasures of plant propagation. Fact is, while most herbs root easily from cuttings, some just don't take well to the water rooting method—and all the magic in the world won't help. The best bet is to root cuttings in sterile soil and treat them much as you did your spring seeds. For real success, though, follow the instructions below. You'll have healthy, sturdy plants in no time flat.

- Fresh, new growth works best for cuttings. Look for healthy foliage on stems between four and six inches in length. Talk to the plant and tell it what you want to do. Wait for an answer. If the plant says no, don't be discouraged. Just go on to another plant.

- Use a pair of sharp scissors or garden shears. Make a diagonal cut just below a leaf node. This is important because the leaf node area is the place new roots will form. As you cut, chant:

> *Have no fear, my little stem*
> *I bring you all the love within*
> *My heart, so you can grow with ease*
> *And be your own plant. Blessed be!*

- Carefully remove any leaves two inches from the bottom of the stem, then dip the stem in rooting hormone. (Rooting hormone is inexpensive and easily obtained from your local garden center.) Chant something like:

> *Leaves fly off and fall away*
> *Make way so roots can sprout today*
> *I dip you in this powder rare*
> *So you'll mature without a care*

- Plant the cuttings in sterile soil. As you plant them, say something like:

> *Little stems so strong and lean*
> *Become new plants—grow lush and green*
> *Form new roots deep in this Earth*
> *And you'll enjoy my garden's girth*

Moisten the soil with water, then care for the cuttings as described in the Protection for Sprouts and Seedlings section in part one.

After a week or two, check the cuttings for root systems. Just give the stem a gentle tug. If you feel resistance, you'll know the root systems have formed. You can then transplant them into their own little pots.

Living Herb Wreath

Another alternative for herb cuttings is to plant them in a living wreath. This option has several perks. For one thing, it's an attractive solution. For another, it handles cuttings and small plants without causing a space problem. Best of all, though, you'll have fresh herbs indoors all year long. They'll be right at your fingertips when you need them, and you'll never have to worry about braving the heat, rain, or winter chill for a clipping or two.

> 1 wire wreath form in the diameter of your choice (I like
>   the type with a top and bottom that snap together,
>   but the single form works well, too)
> Hair pins
> Sphagnum moss
> Sterile soil
> Time release fertilizer
> Floral wire (if you choose the single wreath form)
> Assorted plant cuttings (about two cuttings for every
>   inch of the form diameter)
> Rooting hormone

Fill the form bottom with sphagnum moss, being sure to line the form sides. It's important to leave a distinct indentation in the bottom between the sides, too, because that's where you'll plant the cuttings. Sprinkle the indentation with fertilizer, then fill it half full of sterile soil.

Using the directions and chant above, dip the cuttings in rooting hormone. Then, spacing them evenly, plant them in the soil. (If you have bare spaces, plant a little ivy to even things out. It makes a gorgeous addition to any living wreath.)

When you're satisfied with the planting arrangement, fill the rest of the wreath with sphagnum moss, then use hair pins to secure any trailing plant ends.

If you opted for the single wreath form, wrap the wreath intermittently with floral wire to keep the plants in place. For the snap-together type, just attach the top.

That's all there is to it! Caring for this wreath is a snap, too. Just lay it flat in the bathtub or shower and give it a good soaking when the moss feels dry, then hang it on the shower head or place it over the sink to drain. And once the wreath begins to grow, don't forget to clip it regularly. Clipping not only helps to maintain the wreath shape, but keeps your plants growing green and lush!

Starting Plants by Layering

While you can propagate many herbs with cuttings, those with "woody" stems—rosemary, sage, lavender, and thyme, to name a few—root more easily with a method called layering. During this process, mature plant stems form new plants with separate root systems. I like layering because there's never any wonder or worry. The new sprouts remain in the garden and continue to be a part of the mother plant until they're able to survive on their own.

Layering is one of the easiest propagation methods available to the magical gardener. In fact, I've never seen this technique fail. Best of all, you only need a few things to get started: a razor blade or craft knife, a few hairpins, and the instructions below.

- Locate a healthy, flexible plant branch—one that has new foliage—approximately four to six inches in length. Talk to the plant and get its permission to perform the layering process.

- Using the blade, gently scrape some plant material from the middle of the stem. Be careful not to cut the stem in half. The idea is to create a small wound in the stem so that roots will form quickly. As you scrape, chant something like:

> *Courageous plant, to gain new life*
> *You must brave a little strife*
> *But on your baby's joyous birth*
> *Pain will be lost to love and mirth*

- Bend the stem to the ground, then anchor it with a hairpin. Being careful not to pierce the stem with the pin, push the pin all the way into the soil. Chant something like:

> *New roots form and new roots grow*
> *Sprout new leaves so I will know*
> *When you are able to leave this space*
> *And survive without your mother's grace*

- Heap a little soil over the stem and water it well.

- Brush the soil away every four or five days, and check the stem for new roots. If roots haven't formed, replace the soil, and repeat the chant mentioned above.

- After roots form, allow the stem to stay uncovered. Remove the hairpin and continue to water and nurture the stem until new foliage sprouts. When new foliage is apparent, carefully cut the stem close to the mother plant. Chant something like:

> *This child is ready to leave home*
> *For it can live now on its own*
> *I thank you for a job well done*
> *Live joyously in rain and sun*

Transfer the new plant to its own pot, or transplant it in the garden.

Procreation by Division

Another way to start new plants involves a technique called *division*. It is used on plants—bulbs, peonies, and daylilies, for example—that multiply at a very rapid rate, but don't have the good sense to spread out and take the garden space they need. They just grow one on top of the other until they're all clumped together. This results in an inadequate food supply, improper air circulation, and horribly tangled root systems. Division takes care of the problem by separating the root systems, giving plants some breathing room, and forcing a more even distribution of plant nutrients. This, of course, makes for happier, healthier plants, and allows even the weakest offshoots to thrive and flourish again.

While division is most commonly used for bulb plants, don't discount its virtues for others. Exceptionally large plants or herbs that seem to be taking over your garden are excellent candidates, too. To take back your garden, just follow the instructions below.

- Use a spade to slice around the perimeter of the plant and dig it up. As you slice, chant something like:

> *Roots draw up and roots recede*
> *So I don't cut the ones you need*
> *To live a long and happy life*
> *Away from worry, stress, and strife*

- Shake off the dirt and remove old, dead roots and dead foliage. Then inspect the plant to see if the roots or bulbs of new plants can be separated easily by hand. If so, separate them from the mother plant. As you separate them, chant something like:

> *Little plants, come now with me*
> *So you can grow more easily*
> *With space to roam and more to eat*
> *Let go and live a new life, sweet*

- Using a sharp knife, carefully slice tough-to-separate plants into clumps. Be sure that each clump has both roots and foliage; otherwise, new plants may not fare well. Use the chant above.

- Transfer the new plants to pots or transplant them in the garden. *Note:* If division leaves you with more plants than you can use, give them away to friends and neighbors. They'll be glad to take them off your hands!

Planting Fall Bulbs

Now that you've learned about division and thinned the garden a bit, it's time to plant fall bulbs. This is something you don't want to put off. Why? Because bulbs bring life's cyclical lesson home to us like nothing else. They bloom while the rest of the garden sleeps and lies dormant. They remind us that the cycle of life is ongoing—even in the bitter chill of winter—and that death is merely an illusion. You'll know what I mean the very first time you see them burst through the snow in brilliant colors. It's an experience so uplifting and rewarding that it can't help but put things back in magical perspective.

My mother used to have trouble with bulbs. Sometimes they came up. Sometimes they didn't. It was an iffy situation that left her annoyed, aggravated, and disgusted. Because of this, I spent years shying away from bulbs. I figured that if my mother—the woman with two green thumbs—had difficulty, I should just leave well enough alone.

Years later, I found the source of Mama's trouble. It wasn't the bulbs. The problem lay in the depth of the planting spaces she provided. Some of them were shallow, while others were deep. There was no sense of uniformity. She didn't know that bulbs planted too deeply had no chance of sprouting. And, of course, no one bothered to tell her that one small inexpensive gardening tool could have spared her years of anxiety.

The bulb planting tool is a wondrous device that digs uniformed spaces every time. There's no muss. No fuss. No wondering. You just insert it in the ground and pull it out. The bulb is placed in the hole, covered with soil, and given a good watering. End of problem.

As a result of my discovery, I have gorgeous bulb plants every year. You can, too, if you use the tool and the spell below. Together, they'll guarantee your bulb success year after year.

Bulb Planting Spell

Take the bulbs and planting tool to the garden. Dig the holes, then place the bulbs in the earth while chanting:

Seasons change—the Wheel turns 'round—
Bulbs, I plant you in the ground
Dormant bulbs, you'll come alive,
And when the Spring comes, sprout and thrive

As you cover the bulbs with soil, chant:

Goddess Maiden, dance and play
Upon this soil throughout the day
Crone so wise, so gnarled and old,
Work magical mysteries in darkest cold
Goddess Mother, give them birth—
So they sprout and thrive upon the Earth—
And let them blossom wild and free
The Wheel turns 'round! So mote it be!

Water the bulbs well. Repeat the last chant once a day until the first bulb sprouts.

What if you want bulbs and have no place outside to plant them? Not to worry. You can still grow them indoors. And best of all, you don't have to wait until the fall season to start them. You can enjoy their vibrant colors any time you like with a method called *forcing*. Here's how:

- For indoor planting, try a shallow dish garden pot. These look much like huge saucers and are usually made of terra cotta.

- Cover the bottom of the pot with a thin layer of soil, then arrange the bulbs on top making sure they touch each other.

- Cover with soil until the tops of the bulbs are barely visible while invoking the Crone and chanting something like:

Crone, I plant these in the soil
Make life within them stir and boil
And help them soon to rise and sprout
And blossom in this pot throughout

- Water the bulbs and place the pot in a warm, well-lit area. Add water when the soil is dry to the touch. Bulbs will sprout in just a few weeks.

Putting the Garden to Bed

Like all children, garden plants need quiet time. Unlike human and animal children, though, plants need to rest more than just a few hours. They require the entire winter season to regroup, rejuvenate, and prepare for the spring. It stands to reason, then, that putting the garden to bed may take a little more time as well.

Because harvesting encourages fresh growth, I like to schedule the final harvest about four to six weeks before the first frost. The reason for this is that fresh growth is tender and delicate. It usually doesn't survive the winter months. This time frame gives any new leaves and branches time to gain strength and maturity before they have to brave the cold.

To give plants their best chance for survival, handle the rest of your winter preparations—cutting back, mulching, and so forth—on the first sunny day after the first frost. Go out to the garden and tell the plants what you plan to do. Explain that it's time for them to rest so they can sprout up green and strong in the spring. If you prefer to chant, say something like:

Garden plants, please bend your ears
It's time for bed now, little dears
Close your eyes and yawn and sleep
Draw down into your roots so deep
So that my shears won't cause you pain
And you'll sprout up in the Spring again

After the dew dries, gather some supplies—some rubber bands, a box or basket, a pair of sharp scissors or garden shears, an indelible marking pen, and some labels—and head out to the garden. Start with plants that have rhizomes instead of root systems. (These include oregano, pennyroyal, marjoram, and all mints.) Making diagonal cuts, crop the plants back to one inch above the ground. As you cut, chant something like:

I cut you back now, little one
Beneath the light of shining Sun
So you may sleep through Winter's snow
And wake in Springtime's warming glow

Rubber band the cuttings of each plant together and label them. Then temporarily toss them in the basket or box. You'll want to dry them later.

After you've tended to your rhizomed children, go on to the other plants in your garden. Although you can't cut them as close to the ground as the others, it's perfectly safe to trim away the top two-thirds of each plant. Chant and cut as described above, then band, label, and place in the basket or box with the others. Take the cuttings inside and dry them, using one of the methods described earlier in this chapter.

The next day—or at least before the first snow—hoe the garden thoroughly around and between the plants. This encourages the roots to dig deeper into the ground where they'll be insulated against the freezing cold to come. As you hoe, chant something like:

> *Little roots, run quick and free*
> *Deep inside where cold can't seep*
> *Grow deep where you'll be warm and safe*
> *And Father Winter's ice can't chafe*

Giving the Garden a Blanket

Those of us who live in harsh winter areas don't often think of snow as a luxury. Aside from its aesthetic qualities, we usually associate it with icy roads, broken pipes, and frostbite. Frankly, it's a pain in the butt.

As gardeners, though, we see snow very differently. It's a friend. A loved one. We welcome it with open arms. Why? Because snow prevents fungus and bacteria from growing beneath the soil while plants are dormant. It shields plants from heavy winds, helps to maintain proper moisture balance, and keeps air pockets in the soil from closing up. It provides more insulation and protection than any mulch you can buy.

That's all well and fine. But what if you don't live in a winter wonderland? What if snow is something that only falls every ten years or so? Not to worry. You can insulate your garden against winter's chill with a layer of straw, evergreen boughs, or several layers of newspaper. In lieu of that, a mulch of your choice can be purchased from your favorite garden center.

Winter mulching is easy. Just spread the mulch over the garden area in a layer approximately one to three inches deep, taking care not to cover any plants you've cut back. As you spread the mulch, chant something like:

> *Insulate, protect, and keep*
> *This garden as it drifts in sleep*
> *Keep it warm, secure it well*
> *Until the Maiden rings Spring's bell*

Water the garden, being careful to soak the mulch thoroughly, then give your garden a final blessing by saying something like:

> *Sleep sound, sleep well, sleep long and deep*
> *I entrust you to the Lady to keep*
> *Dream sweet dreams while in Her care*
> *And wake in Spring to weather fair*

Mother Nature's Household

PART TWO

After the Harvest

ALL GARDENERS LOOK FORWARD TO the period just after the harvest. It provides time for some self-appreciation and a well-deserved pat on the back. It gives us a chance to put our harvest to good use and do something creative with our accomplishments. When you get right down to it, it's the only reason we go to all that gardening trouble in the first place. Still, I've met those folks who have no idea what to do with the bounty, much less how to use it to their best advantage. If you're one of those people—or you're running out of ideas—read on. This chapter was written just for you.

One reason we run out of herbal ideas is that we think we already know everything. And why shouldn't we? Everywhere we look, we see magazine articles or books about herbs. We know that we can use them in ritual baths, incense, and oils. We know that we can roll anointed candles in them to boost their powers and use them to asperge Circles. We even know that we can drink them, carry them in our pockets, or wear them to bring about any number of magical possibilities. Since it seems that everything's already been covered then, what's left to know?

Lots!

Fact is, we haven't even begun to tap into the magical possibilities of herbs and their energies. One of the problems is that we've gotten so involved in the "Old Ways" that we've forgotten to update our magic. We seldom make magical use of the everyday tools that make our lives easier. Things like blenders, food processors, Crock-Pots, microwaves, and vacuum cleaners. We've forgotten that herbal magic can alleviate problems caused by insects and dirt just as effectively as it can relieve problems regarding love and money. As a result, we miss out on some of the most potent magic available— magic we could use if we'd just open our minds and let our creative juices flow free. Once we stop stifling the creative force, the magic takes on a life of its own. We suddenly discover that there's nothing we can't do with our herbal friends or their powers.

About the House

When gardeners think of using herbs in the house, their minds frequently conjure up visions of the kitchen, finger bowls, and a gourmet meal. While herbs definitely spice up our food, flavor enhancement is not their most powerful calling. Fact is, they can help us around the house, tend to difficult problems, and save us time. All we have to know is how to use them.

Note: The essential oils contained in dried herbs are more potent than those in fresh. When substituting dried plant material in a recipe that calls for fresh, please reduce the herbal quantity to one-half of the original measurement.

General Enchantment Notes

I'm big on enchantment. Why? Because I believe that refusing to use all available resources is a waste, and magic is one of the most powerful tools in my possession. As a result, I enchant most everything I touch, handle, or use throughout the day. Over the years, it's become a way of life.

For that reason, I also enchant herbs—no matter how I intend to use them— before putting them to work. It's a simple process that adds real oomph to any herbal operation you can imagine. Some of you may already have enchantment formulae that you like to use. If you don't, though, try the tips below. They'll help you get the most from your herbs—and from your magic.

- Place the herbs for the project at hand on the work surface in front of you. (If you're using dried herbs, shake them into a bowl.) Focus intently on the herbs. Feel the power of their energy and vibration flowing about in the atmosphere.

- Lay your dominant hand on the herbs for a few seconds and visualize your need clearly and strongly. Then run your fingers over them (through them, if they're dried). Feel your fingers charging the herbs and infusing them with power.

- When you can feel the herbs tingling with power, remove your hand. The enchantment process is finished.

Herbal Pest Control

HOUSEHOLD PESTS MAKE ME CRAZY. I can't think of anything more annoying than that nagging fly, that buzzing mosquito, or the moth that finds my black wool suit so delectable. Unless, of course, it's the mouse that waits for me in the kitchen with a piece of macaroni firmly ensconced between his tiny paws. Or maybe the weevils that invade my cornmeal, flour, and oatmeal. If household pests drive you nuts, too, don't despair. Try the following tips. They'll make short work of pest-related problems, and leave you with extra time to do the things you want. (The following deterrents contain herbs that are unsafe for children and animals. Please use with caution.)

Ants

Keeping ants out of pantries and cupboards is easy. Just toss in a sprig or two of tansy, rue, or pennyroyal. (Do not, under any circumstances, use pennyroyal if you're pregnant.) As you put the herbs in place, say something like:

> *Ant deterrent, chase away*
> *All critters in this space today*
> *Do your stuff and make them run*
> *As I will, so be it done*

Move the herbs around occasionally, or pinch them to keep the scent fresh.

Then when spring comes 'round again, stop the ant problem before it starts. Just plant some tansy around the house foundation. As you set the plants, chant:

> *Form a boundary, tansy plants*
> *A line that won't be crossed by ants*
> *Keep them out—hold them at bay*
> *Chase any out who stray this way*

If you wait too long and anthills have already formed, sprinkle a little catnip on top of ant paths and mounds while using the chant for cupboards and pantries. Since ants refuse to cross boundaries set by either herb, they'll leave peaceably in search of another place to live.

Flies

Of all the Lady's creatures, none on this Earth cause me more aggravation than the common house fly—especially when I'm up to my elbows in preparing the perfect meal. I find I'm not alone in my disgust. If you have the same problem, try the simple solution below. It not only sends flies packing, but adds a decorative touch to any room in your house.

Make a bouquet, dried arrangement, or potpourri by using any of the following herbs:

Basil, Bay Leaf, Clover Flowers, Elder Flowers or Leaves, Lavender, Mint, Pennyroyal (do not, under any circumstances, use pennyroyal if you're pregnant), Peppermint, Rue, Southernwood

Use as many or as few of the herbs as you like. When you're finished, enchant your herbal fly repellent by saying something like:

> *Herbs of strength, so filled with power*
> *Stand on guard each minute and hour*
> *Repel each fly that comes this way*
> *Hear me herbs! Do as I say!*

Place the bouquet or potpourri wherever flies are a problem.

Mice and Rats

Mice and rats are nervy critters, and often insist on spending the winter in the homes of their human friends. If this happens to you, place small bunches of mint or tansy throughout the house. (Don't forget the attic and basement!) This won't kill the rodents, but will force them to take up residence elsewhere. As you put each bunch in place, say something like:

> *Chase these critters from my house*
> *Get rid of every rat and mouse*
> *Send them packing straight and fast*
> *I command you in the name of Bast*

If this doesn't cure the problem, mouse traps may be in order. For best results, rub the traps with a little anise oil. Another good solution is to bait the traps with peanut butter, then sprinkle on a bit of anise seed or valerian root. As you bait the traps, say something like:

> *Traps be thoughtful—traps be quick*
> *Bait be tasty—do the trick*
> *Do your job efficiently*
> *As I will, so mote it be*

Roaches

When I lived in Texas—a high humidity area—the biggest pest problem in my home involved roaches. Roach bombs were available back then, but because the nasty little critters just ran next door until the fumes cleared, they didn't help much unless my neighbors sprayed their homes at the same time. It was an ongoing battle. Just about the time I was ready to pull my hair out, though, I finally found something that worked. It was so easy, quick, and inexpensive, that I could hardly believe I hadn't tried it before. And all it involved was a few herbs, some water, and a paintbrush!

Start by bringing 2 quarts of water to a boil. Add one-half cup each of dried eucalyptus, rosemary, and peppermint or spearmint. Let the mixture boil for 10 minutes. As it boils, chant something like:

Herbs gain power; mix and blend
Strengthen all you have within
Meld together fast and tight
'Til you become a wash of fearsome might

Remove the pan from the stove and cover it with a lid or plate. Let it sit overnight, then strain out the herbs. Dilute the wash 1:1 with water and mix well. Using a clean paintbrush, apply the solution to baseboards, cupboards, or any place roaches are a problem. As you paint on the wash, chant something like:

Roaches, leave now! Go away!
This wash is deadly to your stay
This herbal potion seals your fate
Go away! Don't hesitate!

Weevils

Weevils are annoying little critters. It's not that they eat so much. They just have a way of turning up unexpectedly—and it's usually in the oatmeal you just prepared for breakfast. Fact is, no grain—flaked, powdered, ground, or chopped—is safe from them. They love it all.

To keep weevils from invading your cornmeal, flour, and oatmeal, grace each container with a single bay leaf while saying something like:

Mighty bay leaf, hear my plea
Keep these contents weevil-free
To their protection you must tend
So they stay fresh for weeks on end

Trash Can Repellent

Normally, I'm a real animal lover. When it comes to overturned trash cans and garbage strewn from one end of the street to the other, though, I begin to have second thoughts. If the neighborhood animals are making a mess with your garbage, don't make a fuss. Just sprinkle the can lids liberally with cayenne pepper and chant something like:

Hot red pepper—fiery stuff—
Make digging through these trash cans tough
Let all who come close feel your fire
And quench all scavenging desire

Flea and Mosquito Repellent

Pennyroyal is not only the best flea and mosquito repellent known to human kind, it's also easy to use. (Do not, under any circumstances, use pennyroyal if you're pregnant.) Just rub the fresh leaves on any part of your body except the face, while saying something like:

Pests, stay far away from me
As I will, so mote it be

For flea problems in the house, scatter dried pennyroyal (do not, under any circumstances, use pennyroyal if you're pregnant) fleabane, or chrysanthemum petals and leaves on the floors—and anywhere else pets may roam—while saying something like:

Fleas, be gone; now get away
Find another place to stay
This home is mine and you must go
As I will, it shall be so

Leave them alone to work their magic for a couple of hours, then vacuum them up.

Moths

Moths definitely have a place in our world. They're graceful, beautiful, and can teach us much about stamina and tenacity. There are lots of places they do belong, but it's certainly not in the closet!

Fortunately, it's easy to keep these fluttering beauties from munching away at your good woolens. Just grab four pieces of net tulle or cheesecloth, and tie up a tablespoon of dried lavender and whole cloves in each. Place them in the four corners of your closet and chant something like:

Herbs of lavender and clove
Let moths not flutter here nor rove
Through my clothes or in this spot
All trace of them, please now erase

Cleaning with Herbs

TO BE HONEST, I ALWAYS knew that herbs had magical, medicinal, and culinary properties. I even knew that they could be used as embellishments for arts and crafts projects. It wasn't until recently, though, that I realized they held power in other areas. An area that made me laugh out loud. Believe it or not, I discovered that herbs were very effective as household cleaning agents.

Fact is, cleaning the house has never been high on my priority list of fun things to do. For one thing, we had a housekeeper when I was growing up and scrubbing just wasn't a part of my life. Of course, things changed as I got older. I had to do my own housework, but only worried about the bare essentials. Truth be told, life was just filled with too much fun to be bothered with something as trivial as scrubbing floors or polishing furniture.

Here's where herbs shine. Just as effective as many products you buy at the grocery store, they're much less expensive. Some of them even cut cleaning time in half. They also give you a chance to flex your creative muscles. But best of all, they're fun to use. And to someone who hates cleaning as much as I do, that's a real bonus!

Household Cleaner Recipes

While I've listed some of my favorite cleaning recipes below, please be aware that herbs can be used to tackle some tough jobs without troublesome mixing, measuring, or infusing. Herbs can freshen air. You can strew dried herbs under door mats and throw rugs, and place them under couch and chair cushions. You can toss a handful of lavender, lemon balm, or mint leaves into vacuum cleaner bags. You can even tie your favorite herbs into a handkerchief and scent your kitchen towel drawer. The possibilities are endless, and only as limited as your imagination.

All-purpose Cleanser

Try this mixture for scrubbing sinks, showers, bathtubs, fixtures, refrigerators, stoves, and kitchen counters. It won't scratch fiberglass or porcelain, and everything it touches shines like new.

- 1 tablespoon baking soda
- ⅓ cup dried rosemary or lemon balm
- 1½ cups water

Microwave the water on high for 4 minutes, then add the herbs and cover with a plate or saucer. Allow to steep for 20 minutes. As the tea steeps, chant something like:

In this water, herbs, gain power
Gain new strength in leaf and flower
We're waging war and dirt is tough
Gather momentum and strut your stuff

Strain out the herbs and stir the soda into the liquid. As it dissolves, chant:

Strongest ally, soda, work
To aid these herbs with grime and dirt
Blend your power strong and sweet
To bring on hasty dirt defeat

Pour into a spray bottle if desired, or apply to dirty areas with a sponge.

Carpet and Upholstery Deodorizer

This little recipe provides the easiest way I know to keep carpets and upholstery smelling fresh and clean. It even works for pet odors. Just sprinkle liberally over carpets and upholstery, wait fifteen minutes, then vacuum up.

1 large box baking soda
1 cup dried herbs of your choice (rose petals, mint, lemon balm, thyme, lavender, and rosemary are all good choices)

Toss the baking soda and herbs in the blender or food processor, and mix well. As it mixes, chant something like:

Herbs and soda, mix and blend
Bring foul, stale odors to their end

Then pour the mixture into a jar with a perforated lid. (Old carpet deodorizer canisters work well for this.) Store any leftover deodorizer in a jar with a tight-fitting lid.

Wood Cleaning Polish

This recipe works well for fine furniture as well as baseboards, windowsills, parquet floors, doors, and other wood miscellanea.

1 can or bottle of oil-based paste soap
½ cup dried lemon balm and/or lavender

Place a fresh coffee filter in the filter cup of the coffeemaker and add the lemon balm. Pour a full pot of water into the coffeemaker and let brew. Empty the soap into a large bowl, then gradually add the tea, stirring constantly to dissolve the soap. As you stir, chant something like:

Properties of soap and herb
Pay heed to this little blurb
Bring splendor back into my wood
And make it shine just like it should

Pour the mixture into a spray bottle and use as furniture polish. Store any remaining cleanser in a glass jar with a tight-fitting lid.

Room Freshener Jelly

Room freshener jelly is not only powerful stuff, but is pretty enough to display anywhere in your house. Best of all, one jar lasts about six months.

- ½ cup bruised fragrant fresh herbs of your choice
- 1 package unflavored gelatin powder
- 1 jelly jar
- ¾ cup boiling water
  Food coloring (optional)
- ¼ cup ice water
  Ribbon (optional)

Place herbs and gelatin powder in the jar, then pour in the boiling water. Stir until the powder dissolves. As you stir, chant something like:

Water, herbs, and powdered gel
Rid this house of nasty smells
Your strength and powers, blend and mesh
To keep the air here clean and fresh

Stir in a few drops of food color if you like, then add the ice water. The mixture will set in a matter of minutes. To make the jar more attractive, tie a bow around the top.

Bath and Boudoir

NOW THAT THE HOUSE IS clean, it's time to relax. And there's no better way to do that than with the help of our herbal friends. Fact is, herbs have a way of transporting us to magical, mystical places—places far beyond the mundane rat race in which we dwell—places where we can destress, deprogram, and just be ourselves. Once we've arrived, things don't seem so difficult. We can sort through problems with an objective eye and find positive solutions that bring goals within reach. And when we do that, we can easily change our personal realities into the lives we'd really like to live. Mere day-to-day existence becomes a thing of the past. And as an added perk, we emerge clean, scrubbed, and refreshed. What could be better than that?

Bronwen's Bath Tub Fizzies

These little gems are a great switch from bath salts. They not only soften skin and smell great, but their fizzy foaming action has a tendency to make folks want to get up and do things instead of just letting life pass them by. Best of all, they can be made with any herbs that suit your magical purpose.

- ¼ cup baking soda
- 3 tablespoons citric acid
- 3 tablespoons powdered sugar or cornstarch
- 3 tablespoons crushed dried herbs of choice (try lavender and chamomile for relaxation, rose petals and clove for love, or chamomile and cinnamon for financial success)
  Small bowl
- 5–6 tablespoons vitamin E oil or almond oil
  Food coloring (optional)
  Ribbon
  Blender
  5-inch square of cheesecloth or net tulle

Blend baking soda, citric acid, powdered sugar or cornstarch, and crushed dried herbs on high speed for 2 minutes, then transfer mixture to a small bowl. Add oil one tablespoon at a time until the mixture is crumbly, but holds together when pressed. As you mix in the oil, visualize your magical purpose and intent, chanting something like:

Herbs and oil and powders mix
'Til my intent is firmly fixed
So when in the bath you finally fizz
My intent becomes what is

Add food coloring if you like, and shape into one-half-inch balls or press firmly into molds (small ice cube trays work well for this). Place on a cookie sheet and bake at 100 degrees for one hour. When cool, check to make sure fizzies are hard and dry to the touch. If not, let them air dry for a few hours.

Place three fizzies in the center of each fabric square, gather the ends together, and secure with a ribbon bow. Use one fizzie bundle for each bath.

Multipurpose Bath Milk

There are few things in life that are capable of transporting you to another dimension more quickly and easily than a milk bath. That's because nothing else feels so rich, so sumptuous, or so luxurious. While this bath can be altered to suit any magical purpose, I find it especially helpful in matters of love and financial gain.

> 2 tablespoons dried herbs (magically appropriate)
> 1 cup baking soda (powdered sugar or cornstarch may be substituted)
> 2 cups dry powdered milk
> Blender
> Flour sifter

Toss herbs into the blender and grind them into a fine powder. Add the baking soda and powdered milk, and blend again. Using the flour sifter, sift the mixture to separate any unrefined plant matter. As you sift, chant something like:

> *Mix of herb and milk so strong*
> *Bring me that for which I long*
> *A multipurpose bath now be*
> *Manifest hopes and dreams in reality*

For best results, add one-half cup of the mix to running bath water. Step into the tub and visualize the dream you wish to manifest.

Personal Empowerment Bath and Shower Soap

In our society, personal empowerment seems to be talked about more often than anything else. At the same time, no quality seems to be more lacking in most of its members; thus, the reason for this soap recipe. It's great for those times when you need a shot of courage, a motivational kick in the butt, or a hefty dose of "I can do anything I put my mind to." Even if you don't think you need any of those things, you still might want to give it a try. Daily bathing with this soap also promotes a sense of self-worth that's beyond compare. And no one can have too much of that, can they?!

        2–3 bars unscented glycerin or Castile soap
         2 tablespoons thyme leaves
         6 tablespoons rosemary leaves
         2 tablespoons lavender leaves or blossoms
         1 tablespoon salt
         3 cups water
            Cheese grater

Grate the soap into a measuring cup, packing it firmly until you have a full cup. Place the herbs, salt, and water in a glass pot and bring the mixture to a rolling boil. As the mixture heats, chant something like:

Herbs of power—herbs of might
Mixed with air, sea, salt, and light
Meld together strong and tight
To take up my empowerment fight

Cover the pot, remove it from the heat, let it stand for 3 to 5 minutes, then strain out the herbs. Pour the soap into the tea, stirring constantly until the soap dissolves. As you stir, chant:

Grated soap and herbal tea
Blend now to empower me
By magic law of three times three
As I will, so mote it be

If the mixture is thicker than you'd like, add hot water in small amounts until it's to your liking. Let cool, bottle, and label.

Worry-Free Garden Shampoo

This shampoo is the best I've found for hair that lacks luster and shine. I've taken this recipe one step further, however, by enchanting it to eradicate incessant worries. Try the chants suggested below, and you can be free of bothersome worry, too.

> ½ cup chopped, bruised herbs (good choices are chamomile, rosemary, lavender, rose petals, thyme, sage, lemon thyme, or lemon verbena)
>
> 3½ cups boiling water
>
> 2½ tablespoons grated glycerin or Castile soap
>
> 1 beaten egg
>
> Glass pot
>
> Wire whisk

Place the herbs in the pot and cover them with boiling water. Cover the pot and set aside for 2 hours. Strain out the herbs and add the soap. Stirring constantly, heat on low until the soap dissolves completely. As you stir, chant something like:

> *Herbs and soap, a shampoo make*
> *For shining hair with every shake*
> *Grant, too, a head that's worry-free*
> *As I will, so mote it be*

Remove from heat and allow to cool. Using the whisk, add the egg and mix thoroughly. As you beat the mixture, chant:

> *Negative energy, fly out the door*
> *Worries be banished forevermore*
> *Bring positive thoughts to me instead*
> *As this shampoo works on my head*

Pour into labeled bottles. Shake well before using.

After-Shampoo Rinse

Try this rinse to promote a feeling of joy, positive energy, and happiness. Just apply it to freshly shampooed hair, then rinse thoroughly with warm water.

½ cup dried thyme
½ cup dried lemon verbena
¼ cup dried rosemary
4 cups vinegar
1 cup water
Old shampoo or conditioner bottles
Blender or pepper mill
Glass pot
Funnel

Using the blender or pepper mill, grind herbs into a fine powder. Place them in the pot, add the vinegar, and allow to simmer on low heat for 15 to 20 minutes. As the mixture simmers, chant something like:

Simmering herbs within this pot
Joy and happiness is your lot
Seal positive energy in your flow
I conjure you now—it shall be so

Remove from heat. When the mixture reaches room temperature, stir in the water and funnel the liquid into bottles.

Herbal Talcum Powder

This powder leaves skin feeling soft and smooth. But that's not all: It's also a powerful weapon against excessive perspiration and the problems it can cause. Even if you don't normally use talcum powder, apply it between toes, legs, and other places where chafing can be a problem. Sprinkle it in your shoes, too, to keep them smelling fresh and sweet.

    2 cups cornstarch
    ½ cup fresh bruised spearmint or peppermint leaves
    3–5 drops essential oil of your choice (optional)
       Plastic zippered bag
       Flour sifter

Place the cornstarch, mint leaves, and oil in the bag, zip it shut, and give it a good shake. Store in a cool, dark area, and shake the bag thoroughly every day for seven days. As you shake, chant something like:

> *Herbs and powder, do your stuff*
> *Mix and meld and blend enough*
> *That your powers join in harmony*
> *As I will, so mote it be*

The fragrance should be strong enough to use by then, but if it's not, store and shake for an additional week. Sift the mixture three times to smooth the powder and separate it from the herbs. As you sift, chant:

> *Soft and smooth and strong now be*
> *Become a warrior instantly*
> *To chase excessive moisture from*
> *The places that it freely runs*

Discard the herbs and store the powder in a clean jar with a screw-on lid. Use a powder puff for dusting.

Love and Romance Lingerie and Linen Sachet

No assortment of bath and boudoir toiletries would be complete without something to scent your lingerie and linens. And what better magical intent than love and romance? It's an age-old commodity that no one ever gets enough of!

- 4 tablespoons dried rose petals
- 4 tablespoons powdered cinnamon
- 2 tablespoons dried lavender
- 2 tablespoons dried thyme
- 2 tablespoons lemon balm
- 1 tablespoon cloves
- 1 6-inch square of net tulle or cheesecloth for each sachet
- 1 9-inch length of red or pink ribbon for each sachet
- 1 small pink candle

  Blender or food processor

Put the rose petals, cinnamon, lavender, thyme, lemon balm, and cloves in the blender or food processor and blend until thoroughly mixed. Place 4 tablespoons of the mixture in the center of each cloth square, then gather the ends together and secure the pouch with the ribbon.

Light the candle and arrange the sachets in front of it.

Visualize the love and romance you desire, seeing it in perfect detail. Then place your hands on the sachets and chant:

> *Messengers of love and romance now be*
> *Find the love and romance that's perfect for me*
> *Deliver your messages quite subtly, but clear*
> *So romance is mine, right now and right here*

Place the sachets in drawers and in linen closets. Replace them once every year. (Instead of throwing the old herbs away at replacement time, try recycling them as carpet deodorizers.)

Dryer Sachet

Ever wish that your laundry could smell as fresh as your herb garden? Or be enchanted for love, personal empowerment, or prosperity? Now it can! Just pack a handful of dried herbs appropriate to your magical purpose into an old sock, and knot the end. As you tie the knot, chant something like:

Herbal wonders, hear my plea
(magical purpose) is what I ask of thee
Bring it now and seal it in
The clothes that dry within this bin

Toss the sock into the dryer. (One dryer sachet will handle about six loads of laundry.)

Herbal Beauty

No MATTER OUR AGES, OUR genders, or our lifestyles, beauty is something we all strive toward. We desire it, cherish it, and work to maintain it. Why? The reason is simple. Silly as it sounds, being beautiful keeps us from feeling old and used up. It makes us feel young, vibrant, and alive. It makes us feel like we belong to the world and that we still have something to contribute. It has a lot to do with the trappings and expectations of the society in which we live.

Regardless of how we feel about that, enhancing our personal beauty is magic at its best. That's because all magic stems from us. We *are* the magic, and any enhancement—whether inward or outward—strengthens our work and adds power to our efforts. Think I'm kidding? Just put on a little makeup and see how quickly people take notice. Wear something sexy and watch the sparks fly. Fact is, making the most of what we have is the quickest way I know to change the way the world perceives us. It also puts the Cosmos on notice that we are serious about our desires and that we'll do whatever it takes to achieve them.

There's nothing wrong with that. Beauty enhancement is simply a matter of reaffirming and strengthening magical intent—one of the most basic components for successful magic.

Please note that there are no magical chants listed with the beauty preparations below. That's because I find it much more effective to bless each set of ingredients before I get started. If this appeals to you, try something like:

> *O Venus, Goddess of Beauty and Love*
> *Look down upon me now from above*
> *Bless these ingredients well and with care*
> *So that they bring beauty beyond human compare*

Lemon Balm Makeup Remover

This little item melts away even hard-to-remove cosmetics like waterproof mascara. It leaves skin feeling smooth and soft, and because it's made with mineral oil, it won't clog pores.

⅛ cup mineral oil
½ cup all-vegetable shortening
¼ cup dried crushed lemon balm
¼ teaspoon powdered orris root (optional—this is a natural
     preservative and keeps the cream from smelling rancid)
Small pot
Jar with screw-on lid

Combine the oil, vegetable shortening, and lemon balm; warm over low heat until the shortening melts. Strain out the herbs, squeezing as much of the oil from them as possible. When the mixture starts to cool, stir in the orris root. Whisk the mixture until creamy, then pour into jars and label. Apply to face with circular motions, then tissue off. (If you decide not to use the orris root, you can keep the cold cream smelling fresh by storing it in the refrigerator.)

Peel-Off Mask

No matter your skin type, no matter your problem, this is the mask for you. It's strong enough to yank impurities right out of their hiding places, but still leaves your face feeling soft, smooth, and fresh.

> 2 tablespoons well-bruised herbs (try mallow for dry
> skin, chamomile for normal skin, and lavender
> or rosemary for oily skin)
> ½ cup boiling water
> 1 package unflavored powdered gelatin
> Small glass pot

Place herbs in a glass pot and pour the boiling water over them. Cover and let steep for 10 minutes. Strain out the herbs and add the gelatin. Heat slowly until the gelatin dissolves. Allow the mixture to cool, then apply it to your face. When the mask is completely dry, peel it off, and rinse with cold water.

Moisturizing Mask

While the peel-off mask is a wonder worker, excessively dry skin calls for some extra attention. That's where this mask comes in. It brings quick relief to flaking skin—even to skin so dry it cracks. It's also a great remedy for faces burned by wind or sun.

> ¼ cup rose hips
> 3 tablespoons plain yogurt

Place the rose hips in a glass pot, cover with water, and bring to a boil. Reduce the heat, cover the pot, and allow to simmer for 15 minutes. Drain the liquid, then purée the hips in a blender or food processor. When the purée cools, add it to the yogurt.

Apply the mask to a clean, dry face. Leave on for 15 minutes, then rinse thoroughly with cool water.

Lemon Balm Toner

Lemon balm toner is the perfect follow-up for makeup remover and mask applications. It not only removes residue and leaves skin feeling refreshed and tingly, but helps to prevent blackheads and other blemishes.

½ cup lemon balm leaves
1 cup boiling water
1 bottle witch hazel

Place the lemon balm leaves in a glass bowl and pour the boiling water over them. Cover the bowl and let the herbs steep for 20 minutes. Strain out the herbs and add the liquid to the witch hazel. Let cool, bottle, and label. For a refreshing treat, store the toner in the refrigerator.

Herbal Moisturizer

Because it's rich in lanolin (the only substance that can penetrate all three layers of the epidermis), this moisturizer works wonders for all skin types. But don't stop at your face. It's great for all-over use, too. Apply it liberally after your bath, a day in the sun, or whenever your skin needs a drink. (Do not apply on broken skin.)

¾ cup fresh comfrey leaves
½ cup fresh lavender leaves and/or blossoms
½ cup fresh rosemary leaves
¼ cup mineral oil
8 ounces anhydrous lanolin

Place the comfrey leaves, lavender leaves, and rosemary leaves in a glass bowl, sprinkle with 1 teaspoon of mineral oil, then bruise them well using a fork or spoon. Set aside.

Heat the lanolin and remaining mineral oil slowly in a glass pan. When the lanolin is completely melted, remove from heat and allow to cool for 10 minutes. Stir in the herbs and allow the liquid to cool for 5 minutes longer.

Strain the herbs from the mixture using cheesecloth or a tea strainer, then pour into jars and refrigerate.

Dandelion Skin Bleach

This little recipe is beauty magic at its very best. Applied lightly twice each day, it removes freckles, age spots, and skin blotches. It even worked on my birthmark!

    12 chopped dandelion leaves
    12 tablespoons castor oil

Simmer the dandelion leaves and oil in a glass pan over low heat for 15 minutes. Remove from heat, cover, and set aside for 5 or 6 hours. Strain out the herbs, then bottle, label, and date.

Peppermint Lip Gloss

This recipe is so easy and inexpensive to make, you may never buy lip gloss again! But what if you want some color? Problem solved. Just melt in a half tube of your favorite lip color when you add the honey.

     6 tablespoons vegetable oil
     1 tablespoon dried peppermint leaves
     1 tablespoon beeswax
    1½ teaspoons honey
        Small cosmetic jars
        Small glass pot

Warm the oil and peppermint on low heat until hot. Remove from heat and cover with a lid or saucer. Allow to cool for 10 minutes, then strain out the herbs. Add the beeswax to the oil and return the pot to the stove, stirring constantly over low heat until the wax melts completely. Remove from heat and add the honey. Blend thoroughly with a spoon or whisk, then pour into jars.

Miracle Cure for Dry, Rough Feet

When it comes to body care, feet are probably the most overlooked area of the body. Why? Because we normally keep them covered with socks and shoes, and seldom expose them to the outside world. Fact is, we just forget about them. Still, feet get a more rigorous daily workout than any other part of the body and need a little extra care. If you've been neglecting your feet, give this recipe a whirl. It's sure to revive your feet and make them the beautiful body part they were meant to be!

1 cup cornmeal
1 cup oatmeal
4 tablespoons salt
2 tablespoons lavender
  Blender
  Plastic zippered bag or jar with lid

Place the cornmeal, oatmeal, salt, and lavender in the blender and process on high for 2 minutes. Apply powder to wet feet and scrub well, being sure to pay some extra attention to calloused areas. Rinse well and follow with moisturizer. Store any leftover scrub in a plastic bag or jar.

Herbal Hygiene and First Aid

Herbs have enjoyed many uses since the beginning of time, but the most common and ancient one, perhaps, is that of medicinal aid and healing agent. There must be something to it, for many of today's prescription drugs still rely on herbal bases. The main ingredient in Valium, for example, is valerian root. The drug digitalis is derived from a foxglove base. (Do not, under any circumstances, ingest foxglove in its natural form. It is not only poisonous, but can be fatal.) Most of the great styptics on the market come from plaintain. The list goes on and on, but one thing is sure: Herbs are still as important and effective today as they were in the time of our ancestors.

The recipes that follow are for minor complaints only, and every effort has been made to ensure their safety for your use. Since every medical case history is different, though—and plant allergies are quite common—please check with your doctor, health practitioner, or medicinal/clinical herbalist before using them.

Aunt Henny's Lip Balm

This little recipe is great for chapped lips, cold sores, and fever blister flare-ups. It also works wonders for dry, cracked cuticles.

> 1 tablespoon fresh sweet violet leaves, chopped
> 1 tablespoon fresh sage leaves, chopped
> 4 tablespoons almond oil
> 2 tablespoons beeswax
> 2 small microwaveable bowls
> Small jar with screw-on lid

Place the violet leaves and sage leaves in the jar, add 2 tablespoons of almond oil, and mix well. Heat in the microwave at 5 second intervals until the scent is noticeable. (The mixture is usually ready when the herbs look as if they've been sautéed and take on a semitransparent appearance.) Set aside.

Place the beeswax and remaining oil in the other bowl. Heat in the microwave at 5 second intervals until the beeswax is completely melted. Strain the herbs from the first bowl and add the infused oil to the beeswax mixture. Beat until cool. Pour into jar, label, and cap.

Powdered Toothpaste

This is a great switch from regular toothpaste. It's inexpensive to make and seems to be capable of reaching areas that normal toothpaste cannot. Best of all, it won't scratch tooth enamel!

> 1 cup baking soda
> 1 teaspoon dill seed
> 1 tablespoon dried parsley
> Jar with tight-fitting lid or plastic zippered bag

Toss the baking soda, dill seed, and dried parsley in the blender and mix well on high speed. Wet toothbrush, dip in powder, and brush teeth as usual. Store in a plastic bag or jar.

Herbal Mouthwash

Tired of mouthwashes that taste like medicine cabinet rejects? Then try this recipe. Not only does it taste great, but it's effective enough to combat even the toughest problems: onion, garlic, and denture odors.

4 tablespoons fresh parsley, chopped
4 tablespoons fresh peppermint or spearmint, chopped
2 tablespoons vodka
2 cups water

Place the parsley, peppermint or spearmint, vodka, and water in the blender and mix well on the highest setting for 3 minutes. Strain out the herbs, then bottle and use.

Upset Stomach Tea

This tea provides quick relief for any minor stomach ailment: queasiness, nausea, or the disturbing feeling that sometimes accompanies the dreaded Saturday morning hangover. It tastes great, too. If you like sweetened tea, try honey instead of sugar.

2 tablespoons fresh ginger root, grated
6 cups water
4 teaspoons dried chamomile flowers
2 teaspoons dried peppermint leaves
2 teaspoons dried lemon balm leaves
Pinch of baking soda
Large saucepan

Place grated ginger root and water in the saucepan; allow to heat on low for 20 minutes. Remove from heat, add the chamomile, peppermint leaves, and lemon balm leaves, and cover. Allow to steep for 15 minutes, then strain out the herbs and drink as needed. Tea may be stored in the refrigerator for up to one week.

Indigestion and Heartburn Tea

If you fall into the "I can't believe I ate the whole thing" category or if heartburn is a problem, give this tea a shot. It whisks away excess stomach acid and brings immediate relief.

    2 teaspoons baking soda
    2 teaspoons anise
    2 teaspoons fennel seed
    2 teaspoons dried dill
    2 cups water
      Bowl
      Jar or bottle with screw-on lid
      Funnel

Place the baking soda, anise, fennel seed, and dried dill in a bowl. Boil the 2 cups of water; pour the contents of the bowl into the boiling water, cover, and allow to steep for 30 minutes. Strain out the herbs and funnel into the bottle or jar. Drink one-half cup as needed.

Store tea in the refrigerator.

Simple Cough Syrup

This syrup is effective and easy to make, yet mild enough for the smallest of toddlers. Given by the teaspoon, it even soothes sore throats.

    1½ cups fresh horehound leaves
      Juice of one-half lemon
      Honey
      Wooden spoon
      Crock-Pot
      Bottles or jars with screw-on lids

Place the horehound in the Crock-Pot and bruise it with a wooden spoon. Then arrange the leaves so they cover the bottom of the pot. Sprinkle them with lemon juice and cover with honey. Cover the pot and, stirring occasionally, cook on the lowest setting for 48 hours. Strain out the herbs, bottle, and store in the refrigerator. Use 1 teaspoon as needed for toddlers and small children. Increase the dosage to 1 tablespoon for adults. (Do not use if pregnant.)

Sunburn Soother

Finally! A sunburn remedy that snuffs out heat, eradicates soreness, and speeds healing. After trying this little remedy, you'll never buy sunburn preparations again!

    4–6 large aloe vera leaves
    ¼ cup fresh lavender blossoms and leaves
    ⅛ cup fresh calendula blossoms and leaves
    ¼ cup vinegar
      Blender or food processor
      Coffee filter

Using the highest setting, mix the aloe vera leaves, lavender blossoms and leaves, calendula blossoms and leaves, and vinegar together in the blender or food processor for 2 minutes.

Strain through a coffee filter into a jar or bowl. Apply the liquid liberally to affected areas. Store any remaining liquid in the refrigerator.

Quick Herbal First Aid Fixes

To Stop Minor Bleeding: Apply a fresh, bruised plantain leaf to the affected area and press firmly.

To Stop Diarrhea: Steep one tablespoon of nutmeg in one cup of boiling water for five minutes. Sweeten with honey if desired, and drink. (Do not use if pregnant.)

To Draw Out Insect Venom and Bring Boils to a Head: Pour two cups of boiling water over one-half cup fresh comfrey leaves (change measurement to one-fourth cup of leaves if dried). Strain through cheesecloth or a four-by-four-inch gauze bandage. Discard the liquid and use the leaves as a hot compress. This is especially effective for spider bites.

To Soothe and Dry Up Poison Ivy or Poison Sumac Blisters: Place one cup of nasturtium leaves and flowers and one-fourth cup of oatmeal in a dry, soft cloth. Gather up the ends and secure them with a rubber band. Toss into a warm bath and use the bundle to scrub affected areas.

Culinary Treasures

BECAUSE HERBS HAVE LONG ENJOYED a place of importance in the hearts of culinary artists, no herb book would be complete without a few tips on using them in food. Fact is, there is nothing that can't be done with herbs in the kitchen. You can sprinkle them on meats, fold them into vegetable dishes, and serve them in drinks. You can mix them into bread, cookie, and pastry doughs, and toss them into quiches. You can even use them as a garnish. Without a doubt, herbs are the most versatile culinary commodity on this planet.

For your convenience, a few of my favorite herbal recipes are listed on the following pages. Give them a shot, but don't stop there. Use your imagination and flex your creative muscles. You'll be serving up delectable palate-tickling masterpieces in no time.

Herbal Vinegars

Herbal vinegars are perhaps the most versatile of all herbal seasoning tools. They can be used to enhance the flavor in a perfect dish and lend spice to a bland one. They are especially great if you got a bit heavy-handed with the salt and pepper. One little sprinkle is all it takes to tone it down.

Because vinegars can be made with any nonpoisonous herb, the recipe below doesn't call for specific species. Try rosemary vinegars for lamb and pork, thyme or sage for poultry, dill or basil for fish, and oregano, garlic, or hot peppers for red meat. Better yet, trust your intuition and work with combinations of herbs. Some of the best vinegars I've ever tasted were born on a whim.

1 cup fresh or dried herbs
1 bottle white wine
   Stainless steel or enameled pot
   Jars with tight-fitting lids
   Candy thermometer

Place the herbs in the pot and pour the wine on top. Heat on the stove until the temperature reaches 110 degrees, then pour into jars and screw on the lids. Place jars in a dark area (kitchen cabinet shelves work well for this). Give the jars a good shake every other day. Open the jars after one week to check the fragrance and flavor. (If either is too weak to suit you, replace the lids and allow the mixture to set up for one more week.) Strain out the herbs and pour the mixture into fancy bottles. Add a sprig or two of fresh herbs if you like, cork, and label.

Grandma Sadie's All-purpose Seasoning Mix

This is the best seasoning mix I've ever tasted. Sprinkle it liberally on meat, fish, poultry, vegetables, eggs, or pizza. Because the recipe makes a large quantity, though, you may want to downsize a bit. In that case, work with tablespoons instead of ounces.

2¼ ounces dried minced onion
2¼ ounces dried thyme
2¼ ounces dried cayenne pepper (for a milder mix,
    substitute sweet red bell pepper)
1 ounce crushed bay leaf
1 ounce dried rosemary
1 ounce dried oregano
2¼ ounces garlic salt
2¼ ounces black pepper
2¼ ounces celery seed
1 ounce salt
1 ounce cloves
1 ounce dried powdered pimento
1 ounce powdered ginger
1 ounce paprika
1 ounce powdered cinnamon
    Postage scale (to weigh ounces)
    One gallon clean dry milk jug
    Blender or food processor

After weighing out the proper amounts, use the blender or food processor to crush the onion, thyme, cayenne pepper, bay leaf, rosemary, and oregano. Use the highest setting for 2 minutes, and only crush about a half ounce at a time (this prevents undue wear on the machine). Pour all remaining ingredients into the jug, replace the cap, and shake well to blend. If you like, fill a few empty salt shakers with the mix, too. This makes seasoning foods a snap during the cooking process.

Rose Geranium Jelly

This versatile jelly isn't just a great addition to toast. Try it on pound cake, mix it into whipped cream or, for a real treat, spoon it into pear and peach halves. After you've worked with this jelly recipe, experiment with other herbs, too. Mint, thyme, rosemary, and lavender are all good bets.

- 4½ cups apple juice
- 1 cup fresh rose geranium leaves
- ½ cup fresh rose petals
- ⅔ teaspoon butter
- 3½ cups sugar
  Candy thermometer
- 2 pint jars with screw-on lids

Place the juice, geranium leaves, and rose petals in a large pot and, stirring constantly, bring them to a rolling boil. Allow to boil for 5 minutes, then add butter and sugar. Still stirring, boil the mixture until it reaches 222 degrees. Remove from heat and strain out the herbs. (Usually herbs rise to the top and can simply be skimmed off with a spoon, but on rare occasions, a thorough straining may be necessary.) Pour into jars and tighten the lids.

Herbal Shortbread Cookies

These are the most delicious cookies I've ever tasted; in fact, they're right up there with chocolate chip! Elegant, rich, and crisp, they are perfect for parties, showers, and luncheons—or for when you just deserve a treat.

- 1 cup butter
- 1 cup sugar
- 2½ cups flour
- 4 tablespoons finely chopped fresh herbs (lemon balm, lemon thyme, sweet violets, mint, or lavender blossoms are good choices)

Cream the butter and sugar, then add the flour. Turn the dough out onto a floured surface and knead in the herbs. Keep kneading until the dough forms surface cracks and no longer sticks to the floured area. Roll out dough to ¼-inch thick and cut into shapes with cookie cutters. Bake on ungreased cookie sheet at 275 degrees until the tops brown lightly—usually about 50 to 60 minutes.

Lavender Thirst Quencher

This drink is precisely what the name implies, for it quenches thirst when nothing else seems to do the trick. Served over ice and garnished with a sprig of fresh mint, it makes the perfect drink for relaxing in the garden.

    1 can pineapple juice
    1 can grapefruit juice
    1 large can frozen lemonade
      Water
    ½ cup dried lavender flowers, crushed
      Large bowl
      Glass pot

Pour the pineapple juice, grapefruit juice, and frozen lemonade into the bowl and set aside. Using the lemonade can as a measuring device, pour 1½ cans of water into the pot and bring to a rolling boil. Remove from heat and stir in the lavender. Cover and let steep for 20 minutes, then strain out the herbs and add the liquid to the bowl. Stir until the lemonade melts completely.

Chill and serve. Store any remaining beverage in the refrigerator. (When stored in containers with tight-fitting lids, this drink keeps for 2 weeks.)

Quick Culinary Herbal Tricks

GARLIC OIL: Place three cloves of minced garlic in an electric potpourri pot and cover with olive oil. Heat in the pot for twenty-four hours, then pour into a jar with a screw-on lid. Brush the oil on meats and vegetables to flavor. Store the oil in your pantry.

HERBED BUTTER: Add four tablespoons of finely chopped herbs to one pound of softened butter, and cream together. Store in the plastic containers and refrigerate. For a festive look, spoon into candy molds and store in the refrigerator until party time.

MINT ICE: Place sprigs of mint in ice cube trays, fill with water, and freeze. Store mint ice in plastic zipper bags in the freezer, then add to cold teas and punches.

SUGARED PETAL CANDY: Brush clean, dry rose or violet petals with egg white, and sprinkle with sugar. Let dry on waxed paper, then store in jars with tight-fitting lids

HERBAL SALT: Bruise two teaspoons of herbs and place them in a salt shaker. Fill shaker with salt, cover with plastic wrap, and replace the lid. Shake three times a day for a week, then remove the plastic wrap and use.

HERBAL CREAM CHEESE: Add one teaspoon of herbs to one package of softened cream cheese. Great on biscuits and bagels!

HERBAL BREAD: Thaw a loaf of frozen bread dough. Knead in two tablespoons of herbs. (For a real treat, add one cup of grated cheese and knead it in, too!) Bake according to package directions. Serve with herbed butter.

Herbs in the Magical Realm

OF COURSE, NO BOOK ON magical herb gardening would be complete without a section of spells and magical projects. When I said something to a friend about writing this portion, though, she just rolled her eyes. The gist of her commentary was that there were a lot of good magical books on the market, and there was nothing I could say that you hadn't already read elsewhere and often. Then she began to pull books from my shelves and point out various examples to confirm her case. She was right. Nearly every book I owned gave the same basic tips on herbal magic. It was the sort of material that, once read and processed, need not be read again.

To that end, this section is a little different. You won't find the same old material, the same tired ritual projects, or the same worn-out herbal notions. What you'll find instead is a combining of ancient ways with modern ones— a meshing of the commonly known and the long-forgotten—and some great ideas to enhance your personal creativity flow. After all, that's what magic's really about!

Who's Herb?
(And Why's He Talking to Me?)

Much like humankind, flowers and herbs speak a language all their own. They whisper in the wind. Their words twirl upon the water. Rooted deep within the earth, their voices gain strength and blossom in the shining Sun. They bid us welcome. They beckon us to listen. They speak of love, betrayal, and good wishes. Their communiqués echo through our spirits like ripples on a pond.

Floriography—the language that our plant friends speak—is a sentimental, peaceful, subtle messenger. It speaks at will and whim about whatever it wants whenever it fancies. It never raises its voice. It never tries to get our attention. As a result, most of its messages go right over our heads. They are, however, captured in the spiritual realm and this is where they can help us.

So, what's all this hubbub about floriography? We've known about plant energies for years. Aren't they the same thing? No. Simply put, plant energy and vibration is what the plant feels like. It has to do with the type of energy that the plant emotes or exudes. This is important to magic because it tells the Universe the kind of spell we're sending, then energizes the spell with the vibrations of our choosing.

Floriography, on the other hand, is the voice of our plant friends. Unlike their human counterparts, though, most individual plants don't have a large vocabulary. Some never say more than a word or two. By combining the voices of several plants, however, we can create a magical sentence that reverberates through the Cosmic Plane.

Used in conjunction with plant vibration, floriography can bring a real boost to spellwork. Together, they give the magical effort energy and definition, a greater chance of Cosmic survival, and the catalyst necessary to bring expedient results and successful manifestation of intent.

For this reason, I like to use both plant energies and florigraphy in my spellcasting. Sound complicated? It's not. All you have to do is decide what message you want the Universe to hear, check the Florigraphy and Magical Associations appendixes in the back of this book, then gather the appropriate plants. If you were working a healing effort for someone with a difficult pregnancy, for example, you might use a combination of tansy, feverfew, thyme, vervain, and lavender. Here's why.

Plant	Language	Magical Energy
Tansy	I declare against you; hope against miscarriage	Health and longevity
Feverfew	Good health	Protection
Thyme	Courage, physical strength	Health and healing
Vervain	Good fortune	Peace, healing, and protection
Lavender	Success	Peace, joy, protection, ease in childbirth

That was easy enough. But now that you've gathered the appropriate plants, how do you apply their messages in spellwork? There are literally hundreds of ways you can use this tool to power your magical efforts. To help you get started, I've listed a few of my favorites below.

TUSSIE MUSSIE: Popular during the Victorian era, these beautiful plant sprig bouquets were sent to friend and foe alike to declare specific messages of feeling and emotion. They are used much the same way in magic. Just enchant the bouquet and send it to the petitioner of the spell, or make one for yourself to instill qualities that seem lacking in your life. The drying process sets the spell. Once it's dry, you can release its magic by charging it for use as a charm and carrying it in a cloth bag, or burning it to carry its message to the Cosmos.

PRESSED PLANTS: Pressed plants and flowers also gained popularity during the Victorian era as a messaging art form that decorated pictures, scrapbooks, and toiletry items. In the magical realm, they can also create an ongoing message to the Universe. Some ideas might include gluing them to spell boxes, Tarot card containers, and candles, placing them between sheet protectors in your Book of Shadows, or arranging them behind the glass of a picture frame. While a flower press definitely comes in handy here, there's no need to fret if you don't have one. Just place the charged plant material between several thicknesses of paper toweling, insert them in a book, and place heavy items on top. Plants are dry in a couple of weeks and ready for use.

INCENSE, OILS, AND INFUSIONS: Floriography can also deliver messages in incenses, oils, and infusions. For incense, just place the dried plant material on burning charcoal. For oils, place herbs in an electric potpourri pot, cover with vegetable oil, and heat for twenty-four hours. Infusions are easy, too. For topical use, just place a tablespoon of each herb in the filter cup of the coffeemaker, add a pot of water, and brew. If you plan to drink the infusion, however, decrease the plant measurement to one teaspoon of each. (Be sure to check a reliable herbal before ingesting any plant material. Some plants are poisonous!)

SIMMERING POTPOURRI: Another way to create an ongoing magical message is to heat charged herbs and water in an electric potpourri pot. In lieu of that, you can simmer them on top of the stove in a saucepan. Don't forget to check the water levels frequently. You may not want your magical message to reach your local fire department!

You get the idea. As you work with floriography and become more familiar with it, you'll find new and exciting ways to apply it. Don't be afraid to use your imagination. Don't be afraid to let creativity take wing. But above all, don't be afraid to listen to that little voice in your head. The herbs that touch your life might just be trying to tell you something!

Magical Herb Lamps

These great little lamps are not only easy and inexpensive to make, but can be structured to fit any magical purpose. They can also double as attractive nightlights.

1 small strand Christmas tree lights in a color
   appropriate to your purpose (about 20 lights)
1 6- to 8-inch round crocheted doily (available
   at arts and crafts stores)
1 jar (quart size or larger)
   Enough dried herbs to fill the jar
   Essential oils appropriate to your purpose
   (optional)
1 2-foot length ribbon in a color appropriate
   to your purpose

Thread the lights through an opening in the doily, then place the lights in the jar. Fill the jar loosely with herbs and sprinkle with essential oils if you like. As you fill the jar, charge the herbs by chanting. In the case of a rose petal love lamp, for example, you might chant something like:

Petals of love and romance true
With your powers this lamp imbue
Spread your energy through my space
And bring the love I can embrace

Thread the ribbon through a circle of evenly spaced holes in the doily while chanting:

The spell is now cast—the circle now sealed
And its magical purpose to the Cosmos revealed

Center the doily over the jar neck and snug up the ribbon ends, tying them securely in a bow. Plug in the lamp. As the lights heat, the scent of your magic will fill the air.

Herbal Beeswax Candles

Want herbal candles, but can't be bothered with the time and mess involved in hand-dipping? Then these are the candles for you! They take only a few minutes to make, but best of all, you won't have to worry about burning yourself or ruining your clothes.

> Essential oil appropriate to your magical purpose
> 1   sheet beeswax for each candle (available at arts
>   and crafts stores)
> 1   candle wick for each candle (available at arts and
>   crafts stores)
> 2   tablespoons dry herbs appropriate to your magical
>   purpose, finely ground (approximate measure)

Rub a few drops of essential oil on your hands, then rub them across the beeswax sheet. As you rub the sheet, visualize your purpose and chant something like:

> *I grease the wheels of magic now*
> *With oil of (magical purpose) and magical vow*
> *So that when lit, my spell will flow*
> *As I will, it shall be so*

Sprinkle the sheet lightly with herbs. (The key word here is *lightly*. A heavy coating of herbs could cause the candle to catch fire in the center when burned.) As you sprinkle the herbs, chant something appropriate to your magical purpose. When making a success candle with lemon verbena, for example, the chant might go something like:

> *Successful herb with lemon smell*
> *Your powers in this wax now gel*

Place the wick on the sheet edge. Roll the beeswax tightly from the edge to form the candle, chanting something like:

I seal you in, O magical power
Increase in strength by passing hour
Until the time I set you free
As I will, so mote it be

Quick Wish Spell

While this spell works well any time during the New to Full Moon, results seem exceptional when it's performed just after the first star of the evening appears in the sky.

Paper
Pen or Pencil
Small bundle of herb stems appropriate to your wish
Yarn or string in a color appropriate to your wish

Write your wish on the paper. Write it completely and in detail, taking care to be specific in the outcome. Wrap the paper around the stem bundle and tie it securely with the yarn, knotting it nine times. As you tie the knots, chant something appropriate to your purpose. In the case of a money spell, for example, you might chant something like:

Money shine and money flow
Money come and money grow
Money come right now to me
As I will, so mote it be

Light the bundle, place it in a fireproof container, and let it burn to ash. Scatter the ashes on the winds within the next twenty-four hours.

Magical Herb Beads

When dry, these easy-to-make herb beads can form any number of magical goodies. String them on jeweler's wire for great Circle headbands. Thread them with drilled stones on doubled beading thread or dental floss for stunning necklaces and pendulum chains. You can even macramé them into today's popular jute chokers or work them into plant hangers. The possibilities are endless.

¾ cup fresh herb blossoms or leaves (destemmed)
6–8 tablespoons all-purpose flour
     Water
     Essential oil (appropriate to your magical purpose)
     Large needle (carpet or darning needles work well)
     Carpet thread or heavy twine
     Blender or food processor
     Bowl

Place the herbs in the blender or food processor, and add a few drops of water. Then process them into puree. (This usually takes 2 or 3 minutes at high speed.) Remove the herbs from the blender cup and place them in the bowl. Add the flour and mix well. Add water one tablespoon at a time until the dough is the consistency of play dough. (If the dough has the elasticity of bread dough, it's too wet. Add a spoon or two of flour to dry it up a bit.) As you mix the dough, chant something appropriate to your magical purpose. If your intent involved increased inspiration, for example, you might invoke the Muses and chant something like:

Muses come from sky and hill
Inspiration now instill
Into this dough that I now blend
Heed my words and power, send

Rub a few drops of essential oil between your hands, then roll small bits of dough into balls for beads. As you shape each bead, chant for further magical enhancement. Using the example above, your chant might go something like:

Creative force and inspiration
Flow within this manifestation

When all the beads are shaped, rub a little essential oil on the thread and knot the end. Thread the needle and string the beads one at a time. Be sure to leave some space between the beads so you can work them back and forth during the drying process.

Hang the bead strings to dry for four days. Slide them back and forth on the string a few times each day to keep them from sticking to the string, while chanting something like:

Air, flow through, around, and about
And seal my magical purpose throughout

When the beads are dry, remove them from the thread. Store in an airtight container until ready for use.

Herbal Paper

Made from herbs to suit your magical purpose, this paper is more fun than you can imagine. You can use it to write love letters and perform money spells. You can use it for special pages in your Book of Shadows or for projects to spark your creativity. The list goes on and on. One note of caution, though: The process is a little messy, so be sure to wear old clothes and allow plenty of time for cleanup.

1 wire coat hanger (or a window screen)
1 pair old pantyhose
  Scrap paper to equal 2 full sheets of newspaper
5 cups water
2 cups finely ground herbs (use a blender, food
    processor, or spice mill for this)
4 tablespoons white glue
  Blender or food processor
  Iron

Start by filling the sink with 6 inches of water. Shape the coat hanger into a square or rectangular form, then stretch the pantyhose mesh over it to make a frame. Set aside.

Tear the paper into small pieces and place it in the blender. Visualizing your intent, add the water and process on low for 1 minute, then process on high for 3 minutes. Pour the mixture into a bowl and stir in the herbs. Mix well.

Place the frame in the bottom of the sink and pour the paper mixture on top. Pour in the glue and knead well with your fingers while chanting something appropriate to your purpose. Your chant might go something like:

Herbs, glue, paper, and water mix
On my intention now well fix
Secure (state magical purpose) in this page
And seal it well for time and age

Lift the frame slowly through the mixture so it's covered evenly. (If you have paper mix left over, you can make more frames and use it now, or pop it in the freezer and save it for later.)

Allow the paper to dry completely, then carefully peel it away from the frame. Iron the paper to flatten it. As this often causes inner moisture to surface, let the paper dry for three additional days before using it. This extra drying time also provides a chance for further enchantment. If this appeals to you, try a daily chant like:

Herbal friends, your powers lend
So (magical purpose) dries right in

Basic Incense Cones

While the recipe listed here makes a terrific all-purpose cleansing and protection incense, it can be easily modified to fit any purpose. All you need are herbs appropriate to your purpose that measure 2 ounces plus 2¼ teaspoons, and 5 drops of essential oil of your choice.

> 5 tablespoons gum arabic
> 6 ounces crushed charcoal
> 1 ounce gum benzoin powder
> ¼ teaspoon powdered sage
> 1 teaspoon sandalwood powder
> 1 teaspoon coriander
> 1 ounce dried bayleaf, minced
> 1 ounce powdered dried lavender
> 5 drops lemon essential oil
> Water
> Food processor or blender
> Waxed paper
> Foil or plastic zippered bag

Mix the gum arabic with a small amount of water to form a stiff paste. Toss the charcoal, benzoin powder, sage, sandalwood powder, coriander, bayleaf, and dried lavender into the blender or food processor and mix on high speed for 30 to 40 seconds. Add the mixture to the paste, stirring thoroughly until blended. Add the essential oil and stir again. As you stir, chant something like:

> *Herbs and gum and water clear*
> *Become protection far and near*
> *So that you cleanse all with your smoke*
> *Your magic powers I invoke*

Form incense cones by rolling bits of the mixture between your hands. (To keep the paste from sticking to your hands, try rubbing a bit of essential oil between your fingers first.) Place cones on waxed paper and allow to dry for 2 or 3 days. Store in a plastic zippered bag or foil to keep them fresh.

Herbal Altar Pentacle

This pentacle is not only easy and inexpensive to make, but the finished product allows you to incorporate herbal and color magic into your efforts on a continuing basis. They also make great gifts. (Since the amount of clay necessary for this project varies according to the desired size of your pentacle, this ingredient amount has been excluded. However, 4 to 5 blocks of clay are usually more than sufficient for a pentacle less than 12 inches in circumference.)

3–4 tablespoons dried herbs of choice (sage, wormwood, patchouli, basil, and mugwort are good choices)
Bakeable clay in your choice of color
Round piece of wood or cork in your choice of size
Cookie sheet
Hot glue sticks and hot glue gun

Using your fingers, thoroughly mix the herbs into the clay while chanting something like:

Herbs of power, meld with clay
Combine your strengths as one this day
Become the power of the Earth
With solid base and joyful mirth

Divide the clay into five equal portions, then form them into long rolls by rubbing them between your palms. Position them on the wood or cork to form a five-pointed star; join and smooth the ends together, trimming if necessary. Remove the star from the round piece and place it on the baking sheet. Chant something like:

Star of herbs and clay and might
Symbol of Earth by day or night
Let magic flow around about
So it is sealed within and out

Bake the star according to package directions. After it cools, hot glue it to the wood or cork.

Absinthe Liqueur

Commonly employed in clairvoyant and psychic work, I also use this drink occasionally for meditation purposes. As its powers are very potent, though, I don't recommend ingesting more than one-half ounce per use. (If you are being treated for any medical condition, please check with your health care practitioner before ingesting.)

- 2 teaspoons crushed wormwood
- 1 pint vodka
- 2 teaspoons chopped angelica root
- 2 teaspoons crushed anise seeds
- ½ teaspoon powdered coriander
- ½ teaspoon fennel seeds
- 4 cardamom pods
-    Quart jar with tight-fitting lid

Pour the wormwood and vodka into the jar, tighten the lid, and shake well. As you shake, chant something like:

> *Fire and herb, meld well and mix*
> *Combine your powers—let them fix*
> *Until the two of your are one*
> *By Moon and Star and Shining Sun*

Set aside for 2 days. Strain out the wormwood and add the angelica root, anise seeds, coriander, fennel seeds, and cardamom pods. Tighten the lid and shake well, repeating the chant above, then allow to sit for 1 week. Strain out the herbs, label, and bottle, chanting something like:

> *Wondrous mix of endless power*
> *Increase in potency with each hour*
> *So that planes and worlds untold*
> *Open and to me unfold*

Place the mixture in a cool, dark place—kitchen cabinets, pantries, or closets work well—to age for 6 weeks.

Magical Herb Wines

The summer that I was eight years old, our pear trees outdid themselves. The fruit was everywhere: on the trees; on the ground; even on the chicken coop. Try as she might, Mama just couldn't bake or can fast enough to keep the fruit from spoiling. Spoilage constituted waste and, in our household, that was unheard of. Daddy finally decided that we'd make some wine—just the two of us—and turn it into a real father-daughter project.

I remember bushels of sliced pears, the scrumptious smell of cloves, cinnamon and lemon, large crocks, and innumerable sacks of sugar. I also remember the steady tap of Mama's foot, her candid remarks about the waste of sugar, spices, and perfectly good fruit, and the muttering under her breath that sounded an awful lot like "fools." Of course, it never occurred to me that Daddy didn't know what he was doing. After all, he was "Daddy," and I thought that word was synonymous with "god"! Fortunately for the two of us, the end result was a big hit. We did so well, in fact, that our winemaking became an annual tradition that lasted until I grew up and moved away.

As wonderful as those memories are, though, I hadn't thought about them in years. It was when I needed something special for a Lammas ritual I was planning that it hit me: There was no reason I couldn't make herbal wine. Not the stuff that you heat up and add herbs to, but the real thing. A full-bodied, homemade herbal brew that Bacchus, Himself, couldn't resist!

Armed with a steady flow of ideas whirling through my brain, I headed for the kitchen. Surprisingly enough, most of the necessary equipment was already in my cabinets. The missing items didn't present a problem, either. With a little imagination, I was able to substitute other ordinary household articles and make a superb brew. By following the instructions on the next few pages, you can, too. The first thing you'll need to do is gather the appropriate equipment.

Equipment

1 4-quart pot
   Large clean plastic bucket or trash can
   Plastic lawn and leaf bags
1 leg cut from an old pair of pantyhose
1 glass jug with a 1- to 5-gallon capacity
   A large funnel
1 large balloon (the neck should be large enough
   to fit snugly around the neck of the jug)
1 siphon (plastic tubing, a piece of garden hose,
   or an aquarium siphon works well)
   Bottles, corks, bottle brushes, measuring
   spoons, and cups

Give some thought to the herbs that you'll use in the wine. For your convenience, I've listed a few good candidates along with their magical properties. But don't stop there. Many others will also work well for wines. Use your imagination and experiment a little. Give floriography some thought. One note of caution, though: Be sure to check a reliable herbal to ensure that an herb you wish to use is not poisonous. No matter how inviting its properties, your magic will fall short in the face of illness or possible fatality!

DANDELION FLOWERS: Imparts the aspects of the Maiden and is excellent for creativity and inspiration, change, and transformational growth.

ELDER FLOWERS: Imparts the aspects of the Lady and is an excellent choice for an all-purpose wine or for use at Full Moon Circles.

LAVENDER FLOWERS: Imparts the aspects of the Crone and can also be used for protection, love, and anger management.

LEMON VERBENA: For success in all endeavors.

PEPPERMINT: For spicing up one's life and bringing excitement to those aspects of living that have become absolute drudgery. (This also works well in relieving the hot flashes caused by menopause.)

ROSE PETALS: For love, harmony, and beauty.

SPEARMINT: To cool raging tempers.

THYME: Imparts joy and relieves depression.

Basic Wine Recipe

    1 ounce dried charged herbs
    2½ pounds sugar
    1 pound chopped raisins
    3 sliced oranges (4 sliced lemons or limes
         may be substituted)
    1 teaspoon yeast nutrient (readily available at
         winemaker's supply stores, but sometimes
         found at a large liquor stores or supermarkets)
    1 package all-purpose wine yeast

Toss the charged herbs into the bucket or trash can and pour 3 quarts of boiling water over them. Cover the bucket with a trash bag immediately and let it sit for 24 hours. After the allotted time, mix 1¼ pounds of sugar and 1 quart of water; heat to a boil. Strain the herbs from the bucket, then add the raisins and sugar water. Let the mixture cool until it's just a bit warmer than tepid, then add the fruit, yeast nutrient, and wine yeast. Cover the mixture with a trash bag, then secure it with string or twine. Stir the mixture twice a day in a clockwise motion for the next 48 hours, chanting something like:

> *Mix and mingle—grow in power*
> *Intensify magic with each passing hour*

Boil half the remaining sugar with 1 pint of water, then let stand until completely cool. Toss it in with the fruit/yeast mixture and let it sit for 48 hours, stirring it clockwise twice each day and repeating the chant above. Boil the rest of the sugar in 1 pint of water, cool, and pour it into the bucket as well. Stir the crock contents twice each day for 3 days, repeating the chant above. (This completes the first fermentation.)

Line the funnel with the stocking, insert it into the glass jug neck, then pour the crock contents into the jug. Remove the funnel and secure the balloon around the neck of the jug. During this process, the wine takes on a life of its own—bubbling and fizzing and dancing within the container. The second fermentation takes at least 6 weeks, so it's an excellent time for further enchantment. Try picking a day of the week appropriate to your magical purpose, lighting a candle of proper color, and enchanting the wine weekly until it's ready for bottling. The ritual you perform doesn't have to be a lengthy one and could be as simple as lighting a candle, some incense, and saying (in the case of dandelion wine):

> *Dandelions, so wild and free*
> *Grant us creativity!*

Remember, too, that visualization and intent are important factors in magical success. For that reason, announce these words with fervor and feeling. Know that you are imbuing the liquid with your intent.

When the wine begins to clear, it's nearly ready. Remove any sediment in the bottom by siphoning the liquid into another bottle. (You might need to perform this process several times.) When the clarity suits you, it's time for bottling. If the wine hasn't cleared within six weeks, though, don't fret! Depending upon the type of wine that's being made, it could take 2 or 3 months for the wine to be ready for use.

Afterword

As I contemplate the wonders of last year's garden—the seeds that became luscious mounds of thyme, soft purple buds of lavender, and glorious yellow and green bunches of pineapple sage—the wonders of my own life come to mind. Wonders of personal growth that came about while doing little more than digging in the dirt.

Yes, I learned a lot during the last growing season—things that only my plant friends could teach me. Things like when to speak, when to be silent, when to take action, and when to retreat. I learned that no matter how much I wanted something—or how badly I thought I needed to make a point—it was sometimes best to just let Nature take Her course. In short, I learned to calm down, relax, and take one day at a time. It's helped me to become a better person.

The most important thing I learned, though, came from watching my garden thrive. You see, herbs don't need much to grow tall and lush and green. And while they like an occasional treat, their very existence doesn't depend on it. Herbs are quite happy with what they have, and know how to put it to good use. They enjoy a simple life. A life where less is more.

That being the case, I've learned to live more like the herbs in my garden. I've weeded out personal belongings. I've cut away excess garbage. I've chopped through the self-imposed restrictions that kept me from being all I could be. And in the process, I rediscovered something that I'd forgotten long ago: the simple, joyful pleasure of being alive in this awesome, wonderful world of ours. It's my hope that you will, too. For in making that discovery, you, like the herb, will become the being you were meant to be—a being like no other—that being who grows lush and green and perfect no matter where you are planted or what life has in store.

Appendix A: Resource Guide to Mail Order Seeds and Plants

ALTHOUGH RELIABLE RESOURCES FOR mail order seeds and plants are springing up everywhere, the following list reflects the businesses I've ordered from and from which I've had exceptional success.

HerBusiness
1798 Post Road East 120
Wesport, CT 06880
(Send $1.00 for catalog and
receive a credit for that amount
on your first order.)

Le Jardin du Gourmet
Box 275
St. Johnsbury Center, VT 05863
(Send $1.00 for catalog and
receive five sample packets of
herb seeds free.)

Logee's Greenhouses
141 North Street
Dept. HC
Danielson, CT 06239
(Send $3.00 for catalog)

Mountain Rose Herbs
PO Box 2000 H
Redway, CA 95560
(Send $1.00 for catalog)

Nichols Garden Nursery
1190 South Pacific
Albany, OR 97321
503-928-9280
(Call or write for free catalog)

Sandy Mush Herb Nursery
Dept. HBC
Leicester, NC 28748-9622
(These folks sell over 1,200 vari-
eties of herbs and perennials.
Send $4.00 for catalog and
receive a credit in that amount
on your first order.)

Appendix B: Monthly Gardening Checklist

ALL AREAS OF THE COUNTRY differ in climate and temperature. For example, the Australian winter falls during the North American summer. Planting times vary from place to place. For this reason, the checklists below reflect numerical, chronological months rather than calendar months. To find month one, just subtract three months from your recommended local planting time.

Month One

- Gather planning supplies
- Locate a suitable gardening space
- Plan garden size and shape
- Order seeds

Month Two

- Start compost heap
- Home Spirit Ritual
- Prepare seedling mix
- Bless seeds
- Prepare seeds (soak, striate, scarify, and so on)
- Start seeds indoors

Month Three

- Tool Consecration
- Prepare garden space for planting
- Thanksgiving Ritual
- Invoke the Spring Ritual

Month Four

- Practice weather-watching
- Obtain a windsock and work with the winds
- Thin seedlings
- Make compost tea

Month Five

- Climatize seedlings
- Plant seedlings and mature plants outside
- Deal with feathered and furry garden pests
- Bless the garden

Month Six

- Fertilize and mulch
- Pull weeds
- Deal with insects and fungus
- Garden meditation

Month Seven

- Harvest the herbs
- Harvest ritual
- Dry and store herbs

Month Eight

- Propagate new plants

Month Nine

- Put garden to bed

Months Ten, Eleven, and Twelve

- Enjoy the harvest
- Plan for next year's garden

Appendix C: Floriography

ACACIA: Friendship

AFRICAN VIOLET: Such worth is rare

ALMOND: Hope

AMARANTH: Immortality, unfading love

AMARYLLIS: Pride, shyness, splendid beauty

ANEMONE: Forsaken

ANGELICA: Inspiration

APPLE BLOSSOM: Preference

ARTEMISIA: Dignity, personal power, poise, dignity, moonlight, sentimental memories, unceasing remembrance

ASTER: Variety, afterthought

AZALEA: Temperance

BACHELOR BUTTONS: Celibacy

BASIL: Best wishes, engagement and betrothal, love, hatred

BAY LAUREL: Artistic achievement, glory, personal accomplishment, reward, success

BEE BALM: Compassion, kindness, your whims are unbearable

BEECH: Money, prosperity, wealth

BEGONIA: Deformity

BELLADONNA: Silence, quiet

BELLFLOWER: Gratitude

BORAGE: Bluntness, courage, directness

BOX: Stoicism

BRAMBLES: Remorse

BROOM: Humility

BUGLE: Cheer, most lovable

BURNET (SALAD): A merry heart, joy

CALENDULA: Affection, constancy, cares, disquietude, grief, health, jealousy, joy, misery, remembrance, the Sun

CAMELLIA: Reflected loveliness

CARAWAY: Don't cheat on me, prevention of infidelity

CEDAR: I live for you

CHAMOMILE: Comfort, energy in adversity, help against weariness, patience, plant physician

CHRYSANTHEMUM: Love, truth

CLEMATIS: Mental beauty

CLOVER: Good luck, good education, hard work, industry

CLOVER (RED): Business, commerce, financial success, industry

COLTSFOOT: Justice shall be yours

COMFREY: Home sweet home

CONEFLOWER (PURPLE): Capability, skill

CORN: Abundance, prosperity, riches, wealth

COWSLIP: Divine beauty

CROCUS: Abuse not

CYPRESS: Death, mourning

DAFFODIL: Regard

DAHLIA: Instability

DAISY: Innocence, beauty

DILL: Irresistible, soothing

DITTANY OF CRETE: Birth

DOCK: Patience

ELDERBERRY: My thoughts are with you, sympathy

FENNEL: Force, strength, thinness, worthy of all praise

FERN: Fascination, magic, sincerity

FEVERFEW: Good health, warmth, you light up my life

FORGET-ME-NOT: Do not forget me, hope, remembrance, true love

FOXGLOVE: Decision, I am not ambitious for myself but for you, insincerity, a wish

FLOWERING REED: I put my trust in God

GARDENIA: Secret untold love

GARLIC: Courage, good luck, protection, strength,

GERANIUM: Comfort, gentility, good manners

GERANIUM (NUTMEG): An expected meeting

GERANIUM (ROSE): Personal preference

GINGER: Comforting, pleasant, safe, warming

GOLDENROD: Encouragement

GRASS: Life is too short

HAWTHORN: Hope

HEATHER: Admiration, protection

HELIOTROPE: Devotion, I turn to you

HIBISCUS: Delicate beauty

HOLLYHOCK: Ambition, fertility

HONEYSUCKLE: Generous and devoted affection, rustic beauty

HOPS: Beer, mirth, rest, sleep

HYACINTH: Unobtrusive beauty, game, play

HYDRANGEA: A braggart

HYSSOP: Cleansing

ICE PLANT: Your looks freeze me

IVY: Friendship, fidelity, marriage

JASMINE: Sensuality, grace, and elegance

JOHNNY-JUMP-UP: Happy thoughts, joyful memories

LAMB'S EARS: Gentleness, softness, support

LARKSPUR: Lightness

LAVENDER: Ardent attachment, devotion, distrust, happiness, luck, soothing the passions of the heart, success

LEMON BALM: Fun, healing, love, relief, rejuvenation, sharp wit, social intercourse, sympathy, understanding

LEMON VERBENA: Attractive to the opposite sex, responsibility

LILAC: Youthful innocence, first love

LILY: Purity, sweetness

LILY OF THE VALLEY: Return of happiness

LOBELIA: Malevolence

LOTUS: Eloquence, mystery, truth

LOVAGE: Strength

MAGNOLIA: Love of nature, perseverance

MARIGOLD: Jealousy

MIMOSA: Sensibility

MINT: Warmth of feeling

MINT (LEMON): Cheerfulness, hominess, virtue

MINT (PINEAPPLE): Hospitality, welcome

MUGWORT: Be not weary, conception, comfort, to overcome fatigue, travel

MYRTLE: Fidelity, joy, home, love, marriage, married bliss, passion, peace

NARCISSUS: Egotism

NASTURTIUM: Patriotism

NETTLE: Cruelty, slander, you are spiteful

NIGELLA: Embarrassment, independence, kiss me twice before I rise, perplexity, prosperity

OLEANDER: Beware

ORCHID: Beauty, magnificence

OREGANO: Happiness, joy

PANSIES: I cannot forget, thinking of you, thoughts

PARSLEY: Feasting, festivity, gratitude, thanks, useful knowledge

PASSION FLOWER: Faith

PENNYROYAL: Flee, go quickly

PEPPERMINT: Cordiality, warmth

PERIWINKLE: Early friendship

PETUNIA: Your presence soothes me

PINKS: Boldness, dignity, fascination, lively and pure affection, fascination, newlyweds, sweetness, taste

PINKS (WHITE): Genius, inspiration, talent

POPPY: Forgetfulness, oblivion, pleasure, sleep

PRIMROSE: Youth, sadness

ROSE (RED): Desire, love, passion

ROSE (WHITE): A heart untouched by love, pure of heart

ROSE (YELLOW): Disloyalty, unfaithfulness

ROSEMARY: Devotion, fidelity, good luck in the new year, remembrance, wisdom, your presence revives me

RUE: Grace

SAGE: Domestic virtue, wisdom, skill, esteem, to mitigate grief

SAGE (PINEAPPLE): Esteem, hospitality, virtue

SAGE (PURPLE): Gratitude

SALVIA: Wisdom, energy

SANTOLINA: Aggressiveness, pursuit, wards off evil

SAVORY: Mental powers

SOAPWORT: Cleanliness

SORREL: Joy, parental affection

SOUTHERNWOOD: Cheerful bantering, jest

SPEARMINT: Warmth of sentiment

STATICE: Never-ceasing remembrance

STOCK: Lasting beauty

SUNFLOWER: Haughtiness

SWEET CICELY: Comfort, gladness, rejoicing, sincerity

SWEET MARJORAM: Blushes, courtesy, consolation, distrust, happiness, joy, kindness

SWEET PEA: Delicate pleasures

SWEET WOODRUFF: Athletic victory, cordiality, eternal life, rejoicing

TANSY: Hope against miscarriage, I declare against you

THYME: Activity, bravery, courage, physical strength, manger herb

TUBEROSE: Dangerous love, voluptuousness

TULIP: Declaration of love, beautiful eyes, hopeless love

VALERIAN: Accommodating disposition, drunk

VERBENA: Family union

VERVAIN: Good fortune, wishes granted, enchantment

VIOLET: Faithfulness, humility, I return your love, loyalty, modesty, simplicity

WHEAT: Abundance, prosperity, riches, wealth

WILLOW: Mourning

WISTERIA: Welcome, fair stranger

WOOD SORREL: Maternal love

WORMWOOD: Absence, affection, bitterness, protection for travelers

YARROW: Healing of wounds, health, to dispel melancholy and heartache, sorrow, war

YEW: Sorrow

ZINNIA: Thoughts of absent friends

Appendix D: Magical Uses of Herbs, Plants, and Flowers

ANGER MANAGEMENT: Almond, Catnip, Chamomile, Elecampane, Rose, Lemon Balm, Lavender, Mint, Passion Flower, Vervain

ANXIETY MANAGEMENT: Skullcap, Valerian

APATHY: Ginger, Peppermint

BEAUTY: Avocado, Catnip, Flax, Ginseng, Maidenhair Fern, Rose, Rosemary, Witch Hazel

BUSINESS SUCCESS: Basil, Hawthorn, Sandalwood, Squill Root

COURAGE: Borage, Cedar, Columbine, Masterwort, Mullein, Sweet Pea, Thyme, Tonka Bean, Yarrow

DEPRESSION MANAGEMENT: Catnip, Celandine, Daisy, Hawthorn, Honeysuckle, Hyacinth, Lemon Balm, Lily of the Valley, Marjoram, Morning Glory, Saffron, Sheperd's Purse

DIVINATION: Camphor, Dandelion, Goldenrod, Ground Ivy, Henbane, Hazelnut, Hibiscus, Meadowsweet, Mugwort, Pomegranate

EMPLOYMENT: Bergamot, Bayberry, Bay Leaf, Pecan, Pine

ENEMIES: Patchouli, Slippery Elm

FRIENDSHIP: Lemon, Orange, Sunflower, Sweet Pea, Tonka Bean, Vanilla

GAMBLING: Buckeye, Chamomile, Pine

GOSSIP MANAGEMENT: Clove, Deerstongue, Nettle, Rue, Slippery Elm, Snapdragon

HEALTH AND HEALING: Allspice, Apple, Barley, Bayleaf, Blackberry, Cedar, Cinnamon, Comfrey, Elder, Eucalyptus, Fennel, Flax, Garlic, Ginseng, Golden Seal, Heliotrope, Hops, Horehound, Ivy, Lemon Balm, Life Everlasting, Mint, Mugwort, Myrrh, Nasturtium, Nutmeg, Oak, Olive, Onion, Peppermint, Persimmon, Pine, Plantain, Rosemary, Rowan, Rue, Saffron, Sandalwood, Sheperd's Purse, Thistle, Thyme, Vervain, Violet, Willow, Wintergreen, Yerba Santa

HEARTBREAK MANAGEMENT: Apple, Bittersweet, Cyclamen, Honeysuckle, Jasmine, Lemon Balm, Magnolia, Peach, Strawberry, Yarrow

HUNTING: Acorn, Apple, Cypress, Juniper, Mesquite, Oak, Pine, Sage, Vanilla

LEGAL MATTERS: Buckthorn, Celandine, Chamomile, Galangal, Hickory, High John, Marigold

LIBERATION: Chicory, Cypress, Lavender, Lotus, Mistletoe, Moon Flower

LOVE: Adam & Eve Root, Allspice, Apple, Apricot, Balm of Gilead, Basil, Bleeding Heart, Cardamom, Catnip, Chamomile, Cinnamon, Clove, Columbine, Copal, Coriander, Crocus, Cubeb, Daffodil, Daisy, Damiana, Dill, Elecampane, Elm, Endive, Fig, Gardenia, Geranium, Ginger, Ginseng, Hibiscus, Hyacinth, Indian Paintbrush, Jasmine, Juniper, Kava-kava, Lady's Mantle, Lavender, Lemon Balm, Lemon Verbena, Linden, Lobelia, Lotus, Loveage, Maidenhair Fern, Mandrake, Maple, Marjoram, Myrtle, Nutmeg, Orchid, Pansy, Peach, Peppermint, Periwinkle, Poppy, Primrose, Rose, Rosemary, Rue, Saffron, Skullcap, Spearmint, Spiderwort, Strawberry, Thyme, Tonka Bean, Tulip, Vanilla, Vervain, Violet, Willow, Wood Betony, Yarrow

LUCK: Allspice, Anise, Bluebell, Calamus, China Berry, Daffodil, Hazel, Heather, Holly, Job's Tears, Linden, Lucky Hand, Nutmeg, Oak, Orange, Persimmon, Pomegranate, Poppy, Rose, Snakeroot, Vertivert, Violet

LUST: Allspice, Caraway Carrot, Cattail, Cinnamon, Cinquefoil, Clove, Damiana, Deerstongue, Dill, Foxglove, Galangal, Ginseng, Hibiscus, Mistletoe, Parsley, Rosemary, Sesame, Southernwood, Vanilla, Violet, Yohimbe

MENOPAUSE: Black Cohosh, Lavender, Peppermint, Sage

MENTAL POWERS: All Heal, Bayleaf, Caraway, Celery Seed, Forget-me-not, Hazel, Horehound, Lily of the Valley, Lotus, Pansy, Periwinkle, Rue, Sandalwood, Spikenard, Summer Savory, Spearmint

NIGHTMARE PREVENTION: Chamomile, Mullein

PREMENSTRUAL SYMDROME: Feverfew, Jasmine, Lavender, Rose

PROPHETIC DREAMS: Anise, Chamomile, Cinquefoil, Cloves, Heliotrope, Jasmine, Mimosa, Mint, Mugwort, Rose, Rosemary, Valerian

PROSPERITY: Almond, Bay Leaf, Basil, Bergamot, Cedar, Chamomile, Cinnamon, Cinquefoil, Clover, Mandrake, Marjoram, May Apple, Myrtle, Oak, Orange Mint, Parsley, Pecan, Pine, Snapdragon, Sunflower, Sweet Woodruff, Tonka Bean, Tulip, Vanilla, Vervain, Wheat

PROTECTION: African Violet, Agrimony, Aloe Vera, Alyssum, Angelica, Anise, Arrowroot, Asafoetida, Balm of Gilead, Basil, Bay Leaf, Birth, Bladderwrack, Boneset, Bromeliad, Broom, Burdock, Cactus, Calamus, Caraway, Carnation, Cedar, Chyrsanthemum, Cinnamon, Cinquefoil, Clove, Clover, Cumin, Curry, Cyclamen, Cypress, Datura, Dill, Dogwood, Dragon's Blood, Elder, Elecampane, Eucalyptus, Fennel, Feverwort, Flax, Fleabane, Foxglove, Frankincense, Galangal, Garlic, Geranium, Ginseng, Heather, Holly, Honeysuckle, Horehound, Houseleek, Hyacinth, Hyssop, Ivy, Juniper, Lady's Slipper, Larkspur, Lavender, Lilac, Lily, Linden, Lotus, Lucky Hand, Mallow, Mandrake, Marigold, Mimosa, Mint, Mistletoe, Mugwort, Mulberry, Mullein, Mustard, Myrrh, Nettle, Oak, Olive, Onion, Parsley, Pennyroyal, Peony, Pepper, Periwinkle, Pine, Plantain, Primrose, Quince, Radish, Raspberry, Rattlesnake Root, Rhubarb, Rose, Rowan, Rue, Sage, St. John's Wort, Sandalwood, Snapdragon, Southernwood, Spanish Moss, Sweet Woodruff, Thistle, Tulip, Valerian, Vervain, Violet, Willow, Wintergreen, Witch Hazel, Wolfbane, Wormwood, Wood Betony, Yucca

PSYCHIC ABILITY: Celery, Cinnamon, Citronella, Elecampane, Eyebright, Flax, Galangal, Honeysuckle, Lemongrass, Mace, Marigold, Mugwort, Peppermint, Rose, Rowan, Star Anise, Thyme, Uva Ursa, Wormwood, Yarrow

SEXUAL HARASSMENT MANAGEMENT: Bergamot, Camphor, Salt Petre, Vervain, Witch Hazel

SLEEP: Agrimony, Chamomile, Cinquefoil, Elder, Hops, Lavender, Linden, Peppermint, Rosemary, Sheperd's Purse, Thyme, Valerian, Vervain

STRENGTH: Acorn, Bay Leaf, Carnation, Mugwort, Mulberry, Pennyroyal, Plantain, St. John's Wort, Thistle

STRESS MANAGEMENT: Calendula, Chamomile, Comfrey, Hops, Lavender, Nettle, Oats, St. John's Wort, Passion Flower, Skullcap

SUCCESS: Cinnamon, Clover, Ginger, High John, Lemon Balm, Orange, Rowan

THEFT: Caraway, Elder, Garlic, Gentian, Juniper, Rosemary, Vetivert

TRAVEL: Bladderwrack, Lavender

VICTORY: Bay leaf, High John, Olive

WISDOM: Hazel, Rowan, Sage, Spikenard

WISHES: Bay Leaf, Dandelion, Dogwood, Hazel, Job's Tears, Sage, Sunflower, Tonka Bean, Vanilla, Vervain, Violet, Walnut

Appendix E: Planetary Rulership

HERBS OF THE SUN: Acacia, Angelica, Bay, Celandine, Chamomile, Chicory, Chrysanthemum, Cinnamon, Citron, Copal, Eyebright, Frankincense, Ginseng, Goldenseal, Heliotrope, Juniper, Lovage, Marigold, Mistletoe, Peony, Rowan, Rosemary, Rue, Saffron, St. John's Wort, Sesame, Sunflower, Witch Hazel

HERBS OF THE MOON: Adder's Tongue, Aloe, Bladderwrack, Calamus, Camellia, Camphor, Chickweed, Cotton, Dulse, Eucalyptus, Gardenia, Irish Moss, Jasmine, Lemon Balm, Lily, Loosestrife, Lotus, Mallow, Moonwort, Myrrh, Poppy, Purslane, Willow, Wintergreen

HERBS OF JUPITER: Agrimony, Anise, Borage, Cinquefoil, Clove, Dandelion, Dock, Endive, Honeysuckle, Hyssop, Linden, Liverwort, Meadowsweet, Nutmeg, Sage, Sassafras, Star Anise, Wood Betony

HERBS OF MARS: Allspice, Asafoetida, Basil, Blood Root, Briony, Broom, Chili Pepper, Coriander, Cubeb, Curry, Cumin, Daniana, Deerstongue, Dragon's blood, Galangal, Garlic, Gentian, Ginger, High John, Holly, Hops, Horseradish, Houndstongue, Masterwort, Mustard, Nettle, Pennyroyal, Pepper, Peppermint, Poke Root, Prickly Ash, Radish, Shallot, Snapdragon, Squill, Thistle, Toadflax, Tobacco, Venus Flytrap, Woodruff, Wormwood

HERBS OF MERCURY: Agaric, Bergamot, Bittersweet, Caraway, Clover, Dill, Fennel, Fenugreek, Fern, Flax, Goat's Rue, Horehound, Lemongrass, Lemon Verbena, Lily of the Valley, Mandrake, Marjoram, May Apple, Mint, Mulberry, Parsley, Peppermint, Pimpernel, Pomegranate, Southernwood, Summer Savory

HERBS OF SATURN: Amaranth, Belladonna, Bistort, Boneset, Comfrey, Datura, Fumitory, Hellebore, Hemlock, Hemp, Henbane, Horsetail, Ivy, Kava-kava, Knotweed, Lady's Slipper, Lobelia,

Mimosa, Morning Glory, Mullein,
Pansy, Patchouli, Quince, Skullcap,
Skunk Cabbage, Slippery Elm,
Solomon's Seal, Tamarind,
Wolf's Bane, Yew

Note: Because much is still unknown—at least herbally—about the planets Neptune, Pluto, and Uranus, these planets have been excluded from the rulership list.

Appendix F: Elemental Rulership

HERBS OF AIR: Acacia, Agaric, Agrimony, Anise, Gergamot, Bistort, Bittersweet, Borage, Bracken, Broom, Caraway, Chicory, Citron, Clover, Dandelion, Dock, Elecampane, Eyebright, Fenugreek, Gota's Rue, Goldenrod, Hops, Houseleek, Lavender, Lemongrass, Lemon Verbena, Lily of the Valley, Linden, Marjoram, Meadowsweet, Mint, Mistletoe, Mulberry, Pimpernel, Sage, Slippery Elm, Southernwood, Summer Savory, Star Anise

HERBS OF FIRE: Alder, Allspice, Amaranth, Angelica, Asafoetida, Basil, Bay, Black Snakeroot, Blood Root, Briony, Carnation, Cat Tail, Cedar, Celandine, Chili Pepper, Chyrsanthemum, Cinnamon, Cinquefoil, Clove, Copal, Coriander, Cubeb, Cumin, Curry, Damiana, Deerstongue, Dill, Dragon's Blood, Fennel, Flax, Frankincense, Galangal, Garlic, Gentian, Ginger, Ginseng, Golden Seal, Heliotrope, High John, Holly, Houndstongue, Hyssop, Juniper, Leek, Liverwort, Lovage, Mandrake, Marigold, Masterwort, May Apple, Mullein, Mustard, Nutmeg, Oak, Onion, Pennyroyal, Pepper, Peppermint, Pimento, Poke Root, Pomegranate, Prickly Ash, Radish, Rosemary, Rowan, Rue, Saffron, St. John's Wort, Sassafras, Sesame, Shallot, Snapdragon, Squill, Sunflower, Thistle, Toadflax, Tobacco, Tormentil, Venus Flytrap, Witch Hazel, Wood Betony, Woodruff, Wormwood

HERBS OF WATER: Adam and Eve Root, African Violet, Aloe, Aster, Bachelor Button, Balm of Gilead, Belladonna, Blackberry, Bladderwrack, Bleeding Heart, Blue Flag, Boneset, Buckthorn, Burdock, Calamus, Camellia, Camphor, Caper, Cardamom, Catnip, Chamomile, Chickweed, Coltsfoot, Columbine, Comfrey, Cowslip, Crocus, Cyclamen, Daffodil, Daisy, Datura,

Dittany of Crete, Dulse, Elder, Eucalyptus, Feverfew, Foxglove, Gardenia, Heather, Hellebore, Hemlock, Hemp, Henbane, Hibiscus, Hyacinth, Indian Paintbrush, Iris, Irish Moss, Jasmine, Kava-kava, Lady's Mantle, Lady's Slipper, Larkspur, Lilac, Lily, Lobelia, Lotus, Lucky Hand Root, Maidenhair Fern, Mallow, Mimosa, Moonwort, Morning Glory, Myrrh, Myrtle, Orchid, Orris Root, Pansy, Passion Flower, Periwinkle, Plumeria, Poppy, Purslane, Ragwort, Rose, Sandalwood, Skullcap, Skunk Cabbage, Solomon's Seal, Spearmint, Spikenard, Strawberry, Sugar Cane, Sweet Pea, Tamarind, Tamarisk, Tansy, Thyme, Tonka Bean, Valerian, Vanilla, Violet, Willow, Wintergreen, Wolf's Bane, Yarrow, Yew

HERBS OF EARTH: Alfalfa, Barley, Bistort, Buckwheat, Cypress, Fern, Fumitory, Honeysuckle, Horehound, Horsetail, Knotweed, Loosestrife, Magnolia, Mugwort, Oleander, Patchouli, Primrose, Quince, Rhubarb, Sagebrush, Tulip, Vervain, Vetivert, Wheat, Wood Sorrel

Appendix 4: Magical Uses of Stones

AMPLIFICATION: Orange Calcite, Quartz Crystal

ANGER MANAGEMENT: Amethyst, Carnelian, Lepidolite, Topaz

BEAUTY: Amber, Cat's Eye, Jasper, Opal, Rose Quartz, Unakite

BUSINESS SUCCESS: Green Agate, Aventurine, Bloodstone, Emerald, Jade, Lapis Lazuli, Malachite, Green Tourmaline

CHANGE: Ametrine, Opal, Unakite, Watermelon Tourmaline

CHILDBIRTH: Geode, Moonstone, Mother-of-pearl

CLEANSING: Aquamarine, Salt

COURAGE: Agate, Amethyst, Aquamarine, Bloodstone, Carnelian, Diamond, Hematite, Lapis Lazuli, Tiger-eye, Watermelon Tourmaline, Turquoise

CREATIVITY: Orange Calcite, Citrine, Opal, Topaz

DEPRESSION MANAGEMENT: Blue Agate, Kunzite

DIETING: Moonstone, Blue Topaz

DIVINATION: Amethyst, Azurite, Hematite, Moonstone, Rainbow Obsidian, Opal, Quartz Crystal

DREAMS: Amethyst, Azurite, Citrine, Opal, Snowflake Obsidian

ELOQUENCE: Carnelian, Celestite, Emerald

FRIENDSHIP: Chrysoprase, Rose Quartz, Pink Tourmaline, Turquoise

GAMBLING: Amazonite, Aventurine, Tiger-eye

GARDENING: Green Agate, Moss Agate, Jade, Malachite, Quartz Crystal

GROUNDING: Hematite, Kunzite, Moonstone, Obsidian, Salt, Black Tourmaline

BAD HABIT MANAGEMENT: Moonstone, Obsidian, Black Onyx

HEALING/HEALTH: Green Agate, Banded Agate, Amethyst, Aventurine, Azurite, Blodstone, Carnelian, Chrysoprase, Coral, Diamond, Flint, Garnet, Hematite, Holey Stones, Jade, Jasper, Lapis Lazuli, Peridot, Petrified Wood, Quartz Crystal, Smoky Quartz,

Sapphire, Sodalite, Staurolite, Sugilite, Sunstone, Yellow Topaz, Turquoise

JOY: Orange Calcite, Chrysoprase, Sunstone, Unakite

LOVE: Alexandrite, Amber, Amethyst, Chrysocolla, Diamond, Emerald, Jade, Lapis Lazuli, Pepidolite, Malachite, Moonstone, Opal, Pearl, Rose Quartz, Rhodocrosite, Sapphire, Topaz, Pink Tourmaline, Turquoise

LUCK: Alexandrite, Amber, Apache Tear, Aventurine, Chalcedony, Chrysoprase, Holey Stones, Lepidolite, Opal, Pearl, Tiger-eye, Turquoise

LUST: Carnelian, Coral, Sunstone, Mahogany Obsidian

MAGICAL POWER: Bloodstone, Orange Calcite, Quartz Crystal, Malachite, Opal, Ruby

MEDITATION: Ametrine, Geodes, Hematite, Quartz Crystal, Sodalite, Sugilite

MENTAL ABILITY: Aventurine, Citrine, Emerald, Fluorite, Quartz Crystal

NIGHTMARE PREVENTION: Chalcedony, Citrine, Holey Stones, Lepidolite, Ruby

PEACE: Blue Agate, Amethyst, Aquamarine, Aventurine, Carnelian, Chalcedony, Chrysocolla, Coral, Diamond, Kunzite, Lepidolite, Malachite, Obsidian, Rhodocrosite, Rodonite, Sapphire, Sodalite, Blue Tourmaline

PEACEFUL SEPARATION: Black Onyx, Black Tourmaline

PHYSICAL ENERGY: Banded Agate, Garnet, Quartz Crystal, Rhodocrosite, Sunstone, Tiger-eye

PHYSICAL STRENGTH: Banded Agate, Amber, Bloodstone, Diamond, Garnet, Cubic Zirconia

PROSPERITY: Abalone, Green Agate, Aventurine, Bloodstone, Chrysoprase, Emerald, Jade, Mother-of-pearl, Malachite, Opal, Pearl, Peridot, Ruby, Sapphire, Staurolite, Tiger-eye, Green Tourmaline

PROTECTION: Apache Tear, Carnelian, Chalcedony, Chrysoprase, Citrine, Coral, Diamond, Emerald, Flint, Garnet, Holey Stones, Jade, Jasper, Lapis Lazuli, Lepidolite, Malachite, Marble, Moonstone, Mother-of-pearl, Obsidian, Pearl, Peridot, Petrified Wood, Quartz Crystal, Ruby, Salt, Staurolite, Sunstone, Tiger-eye, Smoky Topaz, Black Tourmaline, Turquoise

PSYCHIC ABILITY: Amethyst, Aquamarine, Azurite, Citrine, Quartz Crystal, Emerald, Holey Stones, Lapis Lazuli

SPIRITUALITY: Amethyst, Lepidolite, Sodalite, Sugilite

STRESS MANAGEMENT: Amethyst, Chrysoprase, Leopard Skin Agate, Jade, Brecciated Jasper, Paua Shell

SUCCESS: Amazonite, Chrysoprase, Marble

THEFT MANAGEMENT: Garnet, Cubic Zirconia

TRAVEL: Aquamarine, Chalcedony

WISDOM: Amethyst, Chrysocolla, Coral, Jade, Sodalite, Sugilite

Bibliography

Bender, Richard W. "Herb Wines from Scratch." *The Herb Companion*. Loveland, Colo.: Interweave Press, December/January 1993/1994.

———. *The Book of Outdoor Gardening*. Edited by Smith & Hawken Co. New York, N.Y.: Workman Publishing Company, 1996.

Beyerl, Paul. *Master Book of Herbalism*. Custer, Wash.: Phoenix Publishing, 1984.

Bremness, Lesley. *The Complete Book of Herbs: A Practical Guide to Growing and Using Herbs*. London: Dorling Kindersley Limited, 1988.

Brueton, Diana. *Many Moons: The Myth and Magic, Fact and Fantasy of Our Nearest Heavenly Body*. New York, N.Y.: Prentice Hall Press, 1991.

Cunningham, Scott. *Cunningham's Encyclopedia of Crystal, Gem and Metal Magic*. St. Paul, Minn.: Llewellyn Publications, 1987.

———. *Cunningham's Encyclopedia of Magical Herbs*. St. Paul, Minn.: Llewellyn Publications, 1986.

———. *The Complete Book of Oils, Incenses, and Brews*. St. Paul, Minn.: Llewellyn Publications, 1989.

Damrosch, Barbara. *The Garden Primer*. New York, N.Y.: Workman Publishing, 1988.

DeBaggio, Thomas. *Growing Herbs from Seed, Cutting & Root (An Adventure in Small Miracles)*. Loveland, Colo.: Interweave Press, 1994.

Griffin, Judy, Ph.D. *Mother Nature's Herbal*. St. Paul, Minn.: Llewellyn Publications, 1997.

Hutchens, Alma R. *Indian Herbalogy of North America*. Boston, Mass.: Shambhala Publications, Inc., 1991.

Kerenyi, Karl. *Goddesses of Sun and Moon*. Translated from German by Murray Stein. Dallas, Tex.: Spring Publications, Inc., 1979.

Keville, Kathi. *Herbs: An Illustrated Encyclopedia*. New York, N.Y.: Barnes & Noble Inc., in conjunction with Michael Friedman Publishing Group Inc., 1995.

Kunz, George Frederick. *The Curious Lore of Precious Stones.* Copyright 1913 by J. B. Lippincott Company, Philadelphia, Pa.: copyright renewed 1941 by Ruby Kunz Zinsser; published 1971 by Dover Publications, Inc., New York, N.Y. by special arrangement with J. P. Lippincott Company.

Laufer, Geraldine Adamich. "Tussie-Mussies: The Language of Flowers Spoken Here," *The Herb Companion.* Loveland, Colo.: Interweave Press, April/May, 1996.

Malbrough, Ray T. *Charms, Spells & Formulas.* St. Paul, Minn.: Llewellyn Publications, 1986.

Medici, Marina. *Good Magic.* London, England: Mcmillan London Limited, 1988; New York, N.Y.: Prentice Hall Press, a Division of Simon & Schuster Inc., 1989. Secaucus, N.J.: Citadel Press, a Division of Lyle Stuart, Inc., 1971.

Michalak, Patricia S. *Rodale's Successful Organic Gardening: Herbs.* Emmaus, Pa.: Rodale Press, 1993.

Morrison, Dorothy. *Everyday Magic: Spells and Rituals for Modern Living.* St. Paul, Minn.: Llewellyn Publications, 1998.

——— . *In Praise of the Crone: A Celebration of Feminine Maturity.* St. Paul, Minn.: Llewellyn Publications, 1999.

Nahmad, Claire. *Garden Spells.* Philadelphia, Pa.: Running Press Book Publishers, 1994.

Pepper, Elizabeth and John Wilcock. *The Witches' Almanac.* Middletown, R.I.: Pentacle Press, Spring 1994–Spring 1995.

Ritchason, Jack. *The Little Herb Encyclopedia.* Pleasant Grove, Utah: Woodland Health Books, 1995.

Riva, Anna. *The Modern Herbal Spellbook: The Magical Uses of Herbs.* Toluca Lake, Calif: International Imports, 1974.

Stodola, Jiri and Jan Volak. *The Illustrated Encyclopedia of Herbs: Their Medicinal and Culinary Uses.* Edited by Sarah Bunney. Barnes & Noble Inc., by arrangement with Aventinum Publishing House, Prague, Czech Republic, 1996.

Tatroe, Marcia. *Perennials for Dummies.* Foster City, Calif.: IDG Books Worldwide, Inc., 1997.

Tilgner, Linda. *Tips for the Lazy Gardener.* Pownal, Vt.: Garden Way Publishing, a division of Storey Communications, Inc., 1985.

Uyldert, Mellie. *The Psychic Garden: Plants and Their Esoteric Relationship with Man.* Wellingborough, Northamptonshire: Thorsons Publishers Limited, 1980.

Index

Absinthe Liqueur, 149

Basic Incense Cones, 147

Bath and Boudoir:

    After-Shampoo Rinse, 114

    Bronwen's Bath Tub Fizzies, 110

    Dryer Sachet, 117

    Herbal Talcum Powder, 115

    Love and Romance Lingerie and
Linen Sachet, 116

    Multipurpose Bath Milk, 111

    Personal Empowerment Bath and
Shower Soap, 112

    Worry-Free Garden Shampoo, 113

Beauty:

    Dandelion Skin Bleach, 123

    Herbal Moisturizer, 122

    Lemon Balm Makeup Remover,
120

    Lemon Balm Toner, 122

    Miracle Cure for Dry Rough
Feet, 124

    Moisturizing Mask, 121

    Peel-Off Mask, 121

    Peppermint Lip Gloss, 123

Beer Trap, 71

Bulbs, 4, 44, 86–89

Climate:

    Cold Climate Herbs, 12

    Dry Climate Herbs, 13

    Herbs for Shady Areas, 13

    Tropical/Rainy Climate Herbs, 13

    Warm Climate Herbs, 12

Cold Frame, 42–43

Companion Plants, 13

Compost, 17–18, 33, 46–48, 64–65

Compost Tea, 46–48, 65

Culinary:

    Grandma Sadie's All-purpose
Seasoning Mix, 133

    Herbal Vinegars, 132

    Lavender Thirst Quencher, 135

    Quick Culinary Herbal Tricks, 135

    Rose Geranium Jelly, 134

Damping-off, 28

Floriography:

    Incense, Oils, and Infusions, 140

    Pressed Plants, 139

    Simmering Potpourri, 140

    Tussie Mussie, 139

Fungus:

    Chamomile Fungal Remedy, 73–74

    Horsetail Fungal Remedy, 74

    Old-Fashioned Fungal Remedy, 74

Garden:

Balancing, 50–51

Garden Blessing

Harvesting, 3, 76–77, 90

Meditation, 7, 9, 74–76, 149

Preparation, 15, 68–69

Shapes:

Circle, 9

Crescent, 9

Diamond, 9–10

Element Wheel, 10

Moon Phases, 10

Pentagram, 10

Rectangle, 10

Square, 11

Triangle, 11

Wheel, 11

Themes:

Butterfly Garden, 5–6

Culinary Garden, 8–9, 14

Fairy Garden, 6

Gardening Permission, 16

Medicine Wheel Garden, 7–8

Meditation Garden, 7

Moon Garden, 8

Ritual Garden, 6–7, 60

Spell Garden, 7

Sun/Moon Garden, 8

Herbal Beeswax Candles, 142

Herbal Hygiene and First Aid:

Aunt Henny's Lip Balm, 126

Herbal Mouthwash, 127

Indigestion and Heartburn Tea, 128

Powdered Toothpaste, 126

Quick Herbal First Aid Fixes, 129

Simple Cough Syrup, 128

Sunburn Soother, 129

Upset Stomach Tea, 127

Herbal Household Cleaners

All-purpose Cleanser, 106

Carpet and Upholstery Deodorizer, 107

Room Freshener Jelly, 108

Wood Cleaning Polish, 107

Herbal Paper, 145

Herbal Pest Control:

Animal, 18, 90, 102

Ants, 37, 99–100

Flea and Mosquito Repellent, 103

Flies, 37, 56, 100

Mice and Rats, 101

Moths, 103–104

Roaches, 101–102

Trash Can Repellent, 102

Weevils, 99, 102

Herbs:

Drying:

Air Drying Method, 80

Food Dehydrator Method, 80

Gas Oven Method, 80

Microwave Method, 79

Storage, 81

Hydroponics, 46

Insects:

Attractants, 68

Basil Bomber Formula, 70

Fighting Fleabane Formula, 68

Garlic Guerrilla Formula, 70

Repellents, 68
Screaming Banshee Formula, 70
Wormwood Warlord Formula, 69
Living Herb Wreath, 84
Magical Herb Beads, 144
Magical Herb Lamps, 141
Magical Herb Wines, 150
Meditation, 7, 9, 74–76, 149
Moon, 4, 8–10, 30, 36–37, 43–44, 54, 67, 143, 149, 151
Moon Phases, 4, 10, 43
Moon Signs, 4, 43
Mulch, 52, 64, 91–92
Plant Propagation:
    Cuttings, 82–85, 91
    Division, 8, 86–87
    Layering, 85
Purchased Plants, 56–57
Quick Wish Spell, 143
Ritual, 6–7, 16, 19–21, 29, 32–35, 53–55, 58, 60, 77, 95, 137, 150, 153
Rituals:
    Alternative Garden Blessing, 60
    Bird Flyaway Ritual, 55
    Blessing the Seeds, 21
    Bulb Planting Spell, 88
    Garden Blessing, 58, 60

Gardening Permission; 16
Harvest Thanksgiving, 77
Home Spirit, 19–20
Invoke the Spring, 35
Rabbit and Deer Away, 54
Thanksgiving
Tool Consecration, 30, 34
Scarification, 26
Snails, 70–72
Soil:
    Problems, 33, 40, 46, 51, 64, 95–97, 99, 103, 109, 115, 127
    Sterilizing, 22–23
    Stratification, 25
    Strawberry Pot, 45, 47–48, 57
    Thinning, 41, 48
Spell, 5–7, 9, 21, 55, 59, 67, 88, 138–139, 141–143
Tools, 27, 29–32, 39, 96, 132
Transplanting, 43, 45, 48, 57
Tube Trap, 71
Watering, 27, 29–30, 46, 58, 62, 64, 66, 88
Weather Prediction, 36, 39
Weed pulling, 67
Winds, 15, 21, 39–40, 42, 91, 143
Windsock, 29–30, 34–35, 39, 51